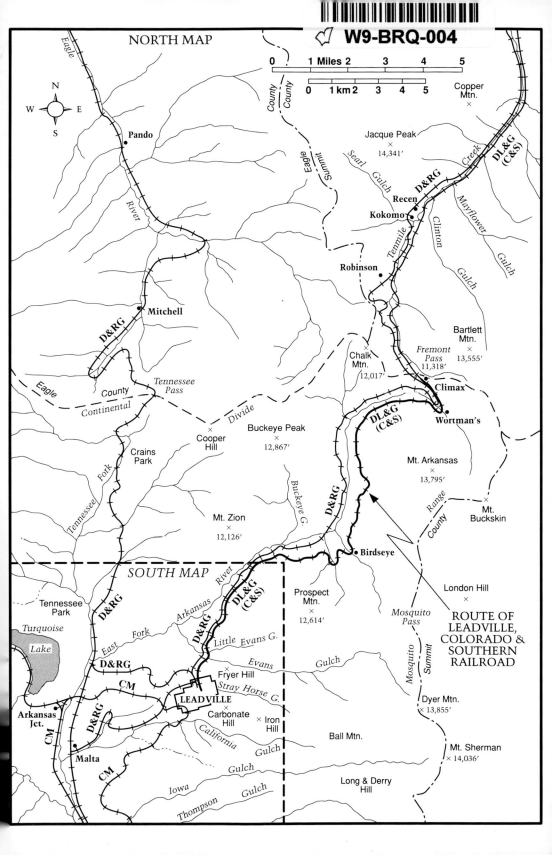

HIGH LINE
to LEADVILLE

A
Mile by Mile Guide®
for the
Leadville, Colorado & Southern
Railroad

by
Doris B. Osterwald

Western Guideways, Ltd.

Publisher – Guidebooks · Railroad and Western History
P.O. Box 15532 · Lakewood, Colorado 80215 · 303/237-0583

International Standard Book Number 0-931788-70-6

Color Separations by
LithoColor
Denver, Colorado

Linotronic typesetting by
National Teleprinting, Inc.
Denver, Colorado

Printed by
Golden Bell Press
Denver, Colorado

To Frank

Among the many legacies
he left his family
is a love of railroads.

ACKNOWLEDGEMENTS

What a sad world this would be without family and friends—especially those who share a love of the out-of-doors and the lore of Colorado's mountain railroads. The list grows with each passing year.

As always, my love and special thanks to each of my family for their support and encouragement. This has been a family project, from beginning to end. Frank and I had started the fieldwork for this book prior to his sudden death in 1989. His beautiful photographs grace the covers and appear throughout. Son Ray, and his wife, April, edited and helped with the field work. Ray also contributed photographs, helped select the final photos, wrote captions, and made sure I had the railroading facts correct. The maps are the result of son Carl's expertise in using Pagemaker and Freehand on the Macintosh. He also handled all the typesetting. His wife, Yvonne, contributed the drawings for the key to conifers and designed the covers. Daughter Becky helped with the layout and editing.

To Stephanie and Kenneth Olsen, my very special thanks for their help and background information on Leadville's new railroad. My thanks also to conductor, Bill Nelson, who treated Ray and me to an unforgettable motorcar ride. His knowledge of mining in the Leadville area was an invaluable resource. Engineer Floyd Leppke and other members of the staff of the LC&S Railroad were always willing and able to answer questions.

I am indebted to Nancy Manly and other staff members of the Lake County Public Library; to Carl Miller, Executive Director of the National Mining Hall of Fame and Museum in Leadville; to Patrick Wadsworth of Climax Molybdenum Co.; and to John Richards, retired engineer at Climax for their contributions. Others who helped in special ways include Ellen and Wally Hansen, Donna Bartos, Gini Seberg, and Jan White.

Charles W. Rische shared memories, photographs, and background information about his grandfather, August Rische. Jack Brenimer related his experiences growing up in Climax during the 1930s, and identified landmarks in old photos of Climax.

To Donna and Rik Collins go special thanks for their help, encouragement, and excellent editing of the geology chapter. Robert W. Richardson, Executive Director of the Colorado Railroad Museum, reviewed the railroading sections for accuracy, as did my railroading friend of many years, Bill Freeman of Sydney, Australia. Final editing was ably handled by Pricilla Patton and Helen Huckenpahler.

Long-time friend Jackson C. Thode offered his friendship and support, and contributed several photos from his extensive collection. Jack and F. Hol Wagner were able to unearth the history of the priceless old D&RG rotary photographs. Hol also contributed photos of the last steam days on the High Line in 1943. Ed Fulcomer's excellent photographs of diesel operations and the French Gulch accident are an important addition to the book, and Dick Kindig's photos tell much about railroading along the route. As always the staff at the Colorado Historical Society, Denver Public Library, and Colorado Railroad Museum were most helpful in finding photographs.

Thanks also to Roland "Gil" Guilkey, a master at making half-tones, and to Richard Hennigar, who ably handled the final layout.

CONTENTS

LIST OF RAILROADS MENTIONED IN TEXT

ASL	Aspen Short Line Railroad (Subsidiary of CM) 1888-1889
AT&SF	Atchison, Topeka & Santa Fe Railroad Co.
B&C	Burlington & Colorado Railroad (Subsidiary of CB&Q)
BN	Burlington Northern Railroad 1970 to present
BT	Busk Tunnel Railway Co. 1890-1893
C&S	Colorado & Southern Railway Co. 1898 to 1981
CB&Q	Chicago, Burlington & Quincy Railroad
CC	Colorado Central Railroad 1869-1890
C&CC	Colorado & Clear Creek Railroad 1865
CC&P	Colorado Central & Pacific Railroad 1866-69
CM	Colorado Midland Railway Co. 1883-1886
	Colorado Midland Railroad Co. 1886-1922
D&NO	Denver & New Orleans Railroad Co 1890
D&RG	Denver & Rio Grande Railway Co. 1870-1886
	Denver & Rio Grande Railroad Co. 1886-1908
	Denver & Rio Grande Western Railway (Utah) 1881-1889
	Denver & Rio Grande Railroad (consolidated) 1908-1921
D&RGW	Denver & Rio Grande Western Railroad 1921-1946
	Denver & Rio Grande Western Railroad (reorganized) 1947-1970
DL&G	Denver, Leadville & Gunnison Railway 1889-1898
DP	Denver Pacific Railway & Telegraph Co. 1867
DSP&P	Denver, South Park & Pacific Railway Co. 1872-1873
	Denver, South Park & Pacific Railroad Co. 1873-1889
GB&L	Georgetown, Breckenridge & Leadville Railway 1881
GN	Great Northern Railroad
KP	Kansas Pacific Railroad
LC&S	Leadville Colorado & Southern Railroad 1987 to present
LMB	Leadville Mineral Belt Railway 1898-1900
MT	Midland Terminal Railway Co. 1894-1949
NP	Northern Pacific Railroad
RGS	Rio Grande Southern Railroad 1889-1952
RGW	Rio Grande Western Railway
UP	Union Pacific Railroad 1867 to present
UPD&G	Union Pacific, Denver & Gulf Railway Co. 1890-1898
WP	Western Pacific

INTRODUCTION

Welcome aboard Colorado's newest passenger railroad, the Leadville, Colorado & Southern (LC&S). For the next few hours, enjoy a leisurely ride on the grade of the former Denver, South Park & Pacific Railroad (DSP&P). The fabled "South Park," also called the "Seldom Punctual," was chartered in 1873.

Construction started from Denver in 1874 and track finally reached Leadville in 1884. The route selected by the DSP&P meandered back and forth, crossing the Continental Divide twice before reaching Leadville, the highest incorporated city in Colorado. One hundred and four years later, the LC&S began carrying passengers on the remaining South Park track between Leadville and Climax.

The LC&S leaves the Leadville depot, elevation 10,200 feet, and gradually climbs a little over 900 feet along the southern side of the upper Arkansas River Valley almost to the summit of Fremont Pass. The route winds through beautiful aspen, lodgepole pine, spruce and fir forests. Travel is slow enough that wildflowers growing along the track may be thoroughly enjoyed, especially during July and August. Other delights of the trip are chances to see deer, elk, coyotes, marmots, rabbits, ground squirrels, pikas, and chipmunks.

Spectacular views of the glaciated upper Arkansas Valley and the high peaks of the Continental Divide make for many photographic opportunities. The open pit of the world's largest molybdenum mine at Climax is also visible from an unusual perspective. Abandoned mine dumps and prospectors' holes left from the mining boom of earlier years stand as forbidding reminders of Leadville's rich heritage.

Between 1884 and 1937, trains carried passengers back and forth to Denver on narrow gauge coaches, and freight trains carried gold and silver ore, coal, lumber, supplies, food and molybdenum concentrates. After 1937, the C&S carried molybdenum concentrates in wooden barrels assembled at Climax. Later, bulk cars and 55 gallon drums were used. Supplies shipped to Climax included bulk cars of caustic, pebbles for grinding (from France and Texas), mining equipment, sodium silicate, pine oil and Dow froth. This traffic lasted until October, 1986, when the last run from Climax was made.

So step back in history and enjoy your trip on the LC&S Railroad, the last remaining section of the old "South Park."

BUILDING THE HIGH LINE

When gold was first discovered in Colorado, mule pack trains carried the bullion across the mountains and through the canyons to the plains and eastern markets. Later, freight wagons made slow, laborious trips back and forth on narrow, rutted "roads." By 1870, when the first railroads reached Denver, mining communities started clamoring for railroads to be built to their towns. Railroads could easily carry heavy mining machinery, equipment, coal, lumber, ores and other freight. Profits from such operations were expected to pay for construction and leave handsome dividends for stockholders.

In 1870, the Denver & Rio Grande Railway (D&RG) was incorporated to build a line southward to Mexico. Management soon realized that it would be more profitable to build into the mountains to the growing mining camps in the San Juan Mountains, Leadville and Aspen. By 1872, the Colorado Central Railroad (CC) started construction up Clear Creek canyon, west of Golden, to Black Hawk, Central City, Idaho Springs and Georgetown. Close on the heels of the D&RG and CC, came the DSP&P with grandiose plans to build through the mountains and continue on to the Pacific coast. These earliest mountain railroads were built *narrow gauge* (rails 3 feet apart) rather than *standard gauge* (rails 4 feet 8-1/2 inches apart), the gauge used by most railroads. This decision was made because narrow gauge construction was cheaper. It allowed smaller engines and cars to go around sharper curves than on standard gauge track. Thus, narrow gauge construction adapted better to mountainous terrain.

In 1873, the DSP&P built southward to Morrison, Colo. to tap coal and lumber available nearby. There was no further construction until the fall of 1876 when the South Park started grading and laying track toward the South Platte River Canyon. From there, the route climbed through the canyon to the summit of Kenosha Pass before descending into South Park at Jefferson. In 1879 track was extended southwestward from Jefferson to Como, the division point. Leaving Como, the mainline continued southwest across South Park to Trout Creek Pass and down Trout Creek Canyon to the Arkansas River at Buena Vista. From there, track was laid westward up a 4% grade to the Alpine Tunnel at the Continental Divide and then continued down more steep grades to reach Gunnison in September 1882.

In 1881 the South Park started building its High Line Extension to tap the riches coming from Leadville, Breckenridge, Kokomo, Robinson, and other mining camps along the way. The route went northwestward from Como, across Boreas Pass to Breckenridge, then westward up Tenmile Canyon to the summit of Fremont Pass. From the top of Fremont Pass, the route wound along the slope of the East Fork of the Arkansas River, to Leadville, affectionately called the "Cloud City" or "Magic City." Leadville was the largest and richest mining camp in Colorado in 1884. At one time Leadville was a candidate to become the State capital.

To understand why the DSP&P selected this route to Leadville, it is necessary to understand the intense competition and rivalry that existed between the DSP&P and the D&RG.

The South Park was anxious to have its own independent route to Leadville so that revenues from carrying ore concentrates, freight and passenger traffic would not have to be shared with its rival, the D&RG. A Joint Operating Agreement was signed Oct. 1, 1879 between the DSP&P and D&RG and was supposed to bring peace between the two railroads. The D&RG was granted the right to build track from Buena Vista to Leadville, and the DSP&P was granted the right to use the D&RG track to Leadville. The DSP&P agreed to pay the D&RG a fee for using the joint track. Profits were to be divided equally. The DSP&P was granted the exclusive right to build a line across Alpine Pass to the Gunnison country, and the D&RG was granted the right to use that track. The D&RG reached Leadville July 20, 1880 and the DSP&P immediately began to use the D&RG track, yards and depot in Leadville. This agreement did not bring peace and harmony, however. During 1880 the two railroads were back in court because the DSP&P believed that the D&RG had broken the Joint Operating Agreement by starting construction across Marshall Pass to Gunnison, so the DSP&P refused to pay the usage fee.

After the UP gained complete control of the DSP&P in early 1881, the UP raised freight rates and miners began to ship their ore from Leadville using the D&RG. By 1882, the D&RG was carrying 85 to 90 percent of the Leadville traffic. The DSP&P (UP), still not paying the D&RG usage fees, realized they had to build their own line into Leadville. In December 1882, the D&RG filed suit against the DSP&P to collect the usage fees. This suit was settled in May 1883 when the DSP&P agreed to pay the D&RG a total of $280,000, or $8,000 per month, for use of the D&RG track from July 1, 1880 to June 1, 1883. Beginning June 1, 1883, the usage fee was increased to $12,000 per month. The two companies also agreed to give each other a 6-months' notice if any change in the agreement was to be made. After this agreement was reached, plans for the last portion of the High Line Extension between Dillon and Leadville were made public.

Construction started Aug. 3, 1883. The August 4th *Leadville Chronicle* reported that the DSP&P had purchased the right-of-way along the Starr Ditch which ran between Hazel and Hemlock Streets from 13th Street to California Gulch. The railroad also obtained an undivided 1/3-interest in the Searle Placer northeast of Leadville. It was reported that three surveying crews were staking out the final location. Contracts were awarded for 50,000 spruce ties and a large amount of rail.

Realizing the DSP&P really was going to build to Leadville, the D&RG cancelled the 1879 Joint Operating Agreement, effective Aug. 6, 1883, and a new railroad war started! This meant the DSP&P needed to complete the High Line Extension before Feb. 6, 1884. By the end of August, the D&RG petitioned the Lake County Board of Commissioners to grant the railroad a right-of-way up California Gulch. This narrow gauge spur track was built to obtain a monopoly on ores from that area. On Aug. 27, 1883, the D&RG also filed a temporary injunction to keep the DSP&P surveying and construction crews from trespassing on the right-of-way of the D&RG Blue River Extension in Summit County, particularly at Kokomo. This injunction also prohibited the DSP&P from diverting any of the water in Tenmile Creek or its tributaries.

Nonetheless, the D&RG turned around and granted the DSP&P permission to use their Leadville roundhouse and yards and also granted two renewals to the Joint Operating Agreement! M.C. Poor, the railroad authority on the DSP&P, believed that, for unknown reasons, there was a certain amount of collusion between the two railroads. Perhaps each railroad knew that floods, avalanches or equipment failures could (and would) make one railroad dependent upon the other.

The C.W. Collins & Company from Omaha, Neb., and Carlisle & Corrigan of Pueblo, Colo., were awarded contracts for grading and construction of the High Line Extension. By Aug. 31, 1883, the UP had transferred a large number of laborers from the Oregon Short Line Railroad. The DSP&P began an active recruiting campaign to attract laborers. Advertisements placed in newspapers in Omaha, St. Louis, Chicago, Kansas City and other midwestern towns for laborers. Men were promised good wages, excellent room and board and plenty of warm clothing needed to work at the high elevations. Leadville newspapers reported that large numbers of laborers were arriving in town. They were sent to various points between Dillon and Leadville. Trackmen were paid $2.25 per day, and rockmen, $2.50 per day; board was $6 per week.

The August 30, 1883 Leadville Chronicle reported:

> A conflict of jurisdiction seems to have broken out between the South Park Railway company and the city authorities. Wednesday a warrant was issued for the arrest of a number of men who were laying the railroad track, but the men desisted from work and were not arrested. It is understood that some of the city authorities had a conversation with some of the South Park officials. The result of the talk, as reported, terminated in the railroad men saying the city could go to hell and they would take the bull by the horns and build their road anyhow....
>
> Officer Roberts says that this morning when he came down town workmen had commenced at Eleventh street and by noon they had laid ties as far as Eighth, when Marshal Cudihee and Officer Roberts went to the place where they were at work and notified all those who had crossed Eighth street could consider themselves under arrest.
>
> ....As soon as they saw there was no foolishness in the matter they all stopped work and threw down their tools. Marshall Cudihee then placed those who had been arrested in front of him and instructed them to proceed down town (and to the city jail), he and Officer Roberts following closely behind.

The men were released from jail the next day. At the regular meeting of the Leadville city council, held Sept. 5, 1883, DSP&P attorney H. B. Johnson reminded the council members that the joint usage of D&RG track would end on Feb. 6, 1884 and that Leadville would then be at the mercy of the D&RG if the South Park track was not completed. He suggested that the city council should promptly enact an ordinance so the DSP&P could lay track across the streets and alleys of Leadville. Ordinance No. 198 was passed the next evening.

Shortly before that fracas was settled, the D&RG parked steam engine No. 6 on the track at the point where the DSP&P had to cross the D&RG spur track to Fryer Hill mines. For several days the engine sat fully steamed, thus preventing South Park construction crews from working eastward toward other crews that were laying track westward from Dillon. This historic location is at present-day milepost 150.5. Later, D&RG crews used the engine to keep an eye on the activities of South Park construction crews.

The next roadblock was yet another court appearance for the DSP&P. A contempt citation was issued against chief engineer James A. Evans, and resident construction engineer P. F. Barr for trespassing on the right-of-way of the D&RG. At the trial, held Sept. 1, 1883, D&RG officials reported that the two men were seen directing water from Tenmile Creek toward the D&RG track. The defendants, when called to testify, said that all surveying on or near the Rio Grande right-of-way had stopped and that they would abide by the law. Contempt citations were dropped, but Judge Moses Hallett of the U.S. District Court made the injunction permanent and called for both railroads to explain their actions. The DSP&P responded promptly, but the D&RG waited until November to reply to the order. At that time, Judge Hallett appointed a commission to report on ways the rails could be laid through Kokomo and still not encroach on the D&RG right-of-way.

Because the D&RG's Blue River Extension was built first, the D&RG secured the most favorable route between Dillon and Leadville. Designing a route through Kokomo was a challenge to DSP&P locating engineers because of the topography of the valley, the location of the town, and D&RG track. In a December 1883 ruling, the commission suggested several ways for the DSP&P to build through Kokomo. Judge Hallett then ruled that the South Park enter and leave Kokomo by building two trestles over the D&RG track. DSP&P locating engineers were unwilling to wait for this decision and in November chose another route that required a switchback above the town. This brought another lawsuit filed by C. S. Stettauer, who owned placer claims on which the railroad wanted to build. Stettauer demanded an exorbitant fee for the right-of-way and even went so far as to build a barricade to prevent any grading on his property. As a result, the railroad deposited $20,000 with the court to guarantee payment when an amount was agreed upon. During the spring of 1884, the court ordered the DSP&P to pay Stettauer $6,000 for the right-of-way. In an interesting turn of events, during the fall of 1884, the South Park Company removed the switchbacks and built the two trestles through Kokomo as previously ordered by Judge Hallett.

It is perhaps ironic that the valley in which Kokomo was located, and the grade for both railroads, are now buried under the tailings ponds from the Amax Company's molybdenum mine!

If legal problems didn't cause enough problems for the South Park, it was soon quite evident that the promises made to attract laborers were not being kept. Newspapers reported that nearly 2000 men had arrived expecting to be provided with adequate shelter, food, and clothing to work at the high elevations during the bitter cold winter. About half the work force was stricken with pneumonia and other illnesses. Hospitals in Lake County were hard-pressed to care for the men. An article in the *Denver Republican* Sept. 11, 1883, described some of the problems the men faced:

> James Connors, one of the patients at the City's poorhouse, was questioned as to the method of his employment and experience. 'You see,' he said, 'we were hired to come here for $2.25 and $2.50 a day. "Mancatcher," that's what I calls 'em. They were the fellows who hired us. We had to pay 'em $2.00 for the hiring. I came from Kansas City. We were to pay $6.00 a week for board. Nothing was said about how we were to be paid. I came and you see I am not a very strong man. I don't know what it is, but the first day I went to work up here in the mountains, I was taken down. I couldn't work, and that night I went to my boss and told him so. My day's wages was $2.25. He couldn't give me the money, he said, and all he offered me was an order on the store for that amount. I took it. What do you think I got? Here it is.' And the laborer took from his pocket a fifteen cent package of Bull Durham tobacco, a ten cent plug, and a five cent box of matches.

Work continued along the route and by January 1884 the railroad was still scrambling to beat the Feb. 6, 1884 deadline. Another skirmish between the two railroads took place at Robinson and was reported in the Jan. 10, 1884 *Leadville Chronicle*:

> **About dark this evening the South Park commenced with about two hundred men to lay (a side) track from their newly constructed line up to and across the Denver and Rio Grande main track, sidings and depot ground of this place (Robinson). The proposed South Park crossing would come within a few feet of the Denver and Rio Grande depot.**

As soon as D&RG's superintendent George W. Cook was notified of this action, he left Leadville on a special train (probably pulled by Engine 6) with about 50 well-armed men. When Cook arrived at Robinson, he ordered two engines placed on the track at the point where the side track had been started by DSP&P crews. He also ordered his men to "hold the fort against all odds." The next day, South Park crews decided not to tempt fate and left to work elsewhere on the line.

As track-laying continued westward toward Leadville, the railroad had to cross the Ingersoll Placer at French Gulch. Sam Boise, representing owners of this claim, secured an injunction and erected a barricade to prevent crews from entering upon the property. Between English Gulch and Dutch Gulch, Richard Finch and Miles Southward, owners of the Old Crown mining claim, also secured an injunction. However, both properties had faulty titles and caused little delay in track-laying.

To meet the Feb. 6, 1884 deadline, the South Park hired extra men to work laying track in and near Leadville. The *Leadville Chronicle* reported:

> **At about 4:30 o'clock yesterday afternoon [February 5] the construction of the new South Park extension from Como to this city was completed. The last spike was driven near Cummings and Finn's smelter (located in Big Evans Gulch), and the ceremony was accomplished by a screaming of locomotive whistles that was perfectly deafening. A few minutes later a special engine and car conveyed a number of South Park officials over the portion of the track where the junction had been completed and the tooting was resumed with *eclat*. Later in the evening the construction trains began to arrive from various parts of the extension, and at 10 o'clock last night four South Park locomotives were at the company's impromptu depot, on East Ninth Street. THE NEW TRACK is pronounced a 'dandy' by the South Park people, while the Rio Grande men shake their heads dubiously when it is referred to. Colonel Horace Newman (one of the attorneys for the DSP&P) says that it is as solid as the Rock of Gibraltar, and that the man who says the ties are embedded in snow is a bold liar. 'The ties were laid before the snow began to fall' said Colonel Newman to a reporter last night, 'and the track will bear any weight it may be called upon to sustain....'"**

The Feb. 1, 1884 *Leadville Chronicle* reported that the D&RG, CB&Q, AT&SF, CP and UP had reached an agreement whereby all companies agreed to charge the same freight rate and not cut prices. The newspaper believed that this agreement would lessen the rivalry and competition between the DSP&P (UP) and D&RG.

Troubles still plagued the South Park, however. On Feb. 1, 1884 the Leadville roundhouse, used jointly by the two railroads, was destroyed by fire; five D&RG locomotives and one DSP&P locomotive were badly damaged.

During February and March, fierce winter snows blocked railroads all over the State, and the DSP&P was unable to run any work trains over the line. Even the D&RG's Blue River Extension had major problems staying open. The DSP&P was forced to request an extension of the Joint Operating Agreement to May 1. When snow began to melt, crews found that the new unballasted track was washed out in many places and the company was forced to seek a second extension. Finally in July crews were able to start work on the track. (The D&RG was more than willing to grant this extension because the company was heavily in debt and went into receivership July 12, 1884.)

Banner headlines in the *Leadville Morning Democrat* of Sept. 30, 1884, announced the High Line was finally complete and ready for business.

> **The Denver, South Park and Pacific Railroad company will commence running trains over the High Line this morning, saving one hour and five minutes in the time between Leadville and Denver.... With completion of the new route the South Park will be independent of its rival, except as hereafter noted, and will have its own Leadville depot and offices. The corporation has erected, on the corner of Ninth and Hemlock streets, a handsome and commodious freight depot, and has purchased and remodeled a dwelling at 327 East Eighth street for temporary use as a passenger station. This building is excellently arranged for the purpose, and, as adapted, contains ladies' and gentlemen's waiting rooms, with a large baggage room in the rear, and plenty of room on the second floor for operator and clerks. The first train for Denver over the new road will leave Leadville at 8:45 this morning and arrive at the Queen City at 6:15 this evening.**
>
> **There will be two freight trains a day each way over the new line, the evening freight from Denver reaching Leadville for delivery at 10 o'clock the next morning, a gain of seven hours time....**
>
> **From Denver to Leadville by the old South Park line is 171 miles; by the new line it is 151 miles, and by the Denver and Rio Grande road, by way of Pueblo and Colorado Springs, 277 and 4-10 miles....A new turn table and a water tank has been put in for the South Park's use.**

Special excursions were always an important—and fun—way to publicize the completion of a new route, and the section of the High Line between Leadville and Breckenridge was no exception. On Sunday Oct. 26, 1884, two trains left the Leadville depot bound for Breckenridge where a gala celebration and picnic were

The first DSP&P Leadville depot in 1892.
  (Gilbert & Casey photo, Colorado Historical Society)

planned. The regular morning train left the Leadville depot at 8 a.m. with two extra chair cars and pulled by two locomotives. An excursion train left Leadville 20 minutes later, running as a second section of the regular train. It was also double-headed. This second train stopped at Robinson and Kokomo for additional passengers. Even a cold, wet snow did not dampen the enthusiasm of the 400 to 500 hundred passengers who made the trip that day. As reported in the Oct. 27, 1884 *Leadville Chronicle:*

> At 8 a.m. as the excursionists assembled at the depot, a few of them had qualms about boarding the train when they saw Doc Holliday on the platform, however, these feeling were dispelled after it became evident the sporting fraternity was to be represented by such men as the popular Pap Wyman [a Leadville businessman] rather than those of the anti-Holliday faction....
>
> The excursion was under the general supervision of. D. L. Sturgis, traveling agent of the Union Pacific. Every detail was attended to, and every attention paid to the comfort of the passengers. The unpropitious weather disarranged plans somewhat, as the excursion was expected to remain in Breckenridge until 7 o'clock in the evening, but to avoid an entire night ride homeward the time was changed to 4 o'clock....
>
> The people of Breckenridge were ready with plenty to eat and drink, and while they are $1,000 ahead, every one went away satisfied....
>
> Much of the natural scenery of the High Line was hidden by the blinding snow, but occasionally, the train appeared above the clouds, as at Birdseye, where the view was indescribable....
>
> At 7 o'clock last evening every excursionist was at home, with nothing but the weather to have marred a day of pleasure....

The total cost of building the High Line Extension between Como and Leadville was $1,134,399.59 or $18,000 per mile, according to M.C. Poor (1976, p. 265). Total cost of the Dillon to Leadville segment is not known. Even though the DSP&P chose routes that were shorter than those of the D&RG, construction costs were much higher because the company insisted on well-built, permanent grades. The D&RG used cheaper grading techniques and wooden trestles which required much more maintenance. These costs were never recovered by the DSP&P because the mining boom in Leadville peaked in 1883, shippers continued using the D&RG, and the cost of operating a railroad across Boreas and Fremont Passes was astronomical. The cost of additional helper engines, coupled with the problems of keeping the line open during the frigid winter months also added to a negative balance sheet. Another factor was the additional competition the standard gauge Colorado Midland (CM) brought to the Leadville market starting in 1887.

Because the DSP&P had failed to earn even its bond interest after 1883 the railroad was placed in receivership in May 1888. This was partly due to mis-management by the UP, who completely controlled the DSP&P. In 1889, the company was reorganized and renamed the Denver, Leadville & Gunnison Railroad (DL&G), (but still affectionately called the South Park). The railroad remained under the complete control of the UP, however. Despite continued financial woes, the DL&G managed to buy eight new narrow gauge locomotives in 1890. Engine No. 69 (photo, p. 138) was one of these new engines.

It seems incongruous that the UP would finance and build a new depot in Leadville, but construction of a brick and sandstone building started in June 1892 and was completed in January 1893. The new depot (the present LC&S depot) had an office, separate ladies' and gentlemen's waiting rooms and a baggage room. As reported in the *Leadville Evening Chronicle* in January 1893:

> **The clerks of the Union Pacific system in this city have at last been enabled to leave their rickety quarters in the old depot which they have occupied since the South Park entered the city....**
>
> **The wainscoating [sic] [wooden paneling on the walls] and flooring of the new waiting rooms and offices are finished in Texas Pine, and the walls and ceilings are finished in kalsomine over several heavy coats of plaster. The settees in the waiting rooms have perforated backs and seats with brass divisions. These rooms are heated by handsome base burners, in which is used hard coal. The ticket office is small but sufficiently large for the business. It is fitted up with new ticket cabinets, and will also contain a private desk for the cashier, T. B. Dean. The business or main office contains five desks for the clerks and dispatcher, whose window opens into the gentlemen's waiting room. The baggage room adjoins the business office. Dr. Dean has two rooms in the upper story, which have been nicely fitted up for his own private use. The building will be lighted by electricity, and the waiting rooms are hung with brass chandeliers.**

In 1898 the DL&G, still in financial straits, was sold in foreclosure and became one of the narrow gauge routes of the Colorado & Southern Railway Co. (C&S). That same year the C&S was acquired by the Chicago Burlington & Quincy (CB&Q), but retained its C&S identity. The C&S operated its narrow gauge branches until the late 1930s when all the routes were dismantled, except for the High Line between Climax and Leadville.

This 13.7 miles of track was saved because freight traffic from the Climax Mine was too high to justify abandonment. Molybdenum concentrates from Climax were shipped to Leadville and on to Eastern markets via the standard gauge Denver & Rio Grande Western Railroad connection. In 1943 the High Line was converted to standard gauge so that freight did not have to be transferred to and from narrow gauge cars.

The CB&Q (owner of the C&S) was merged with the new Burlington Northern Railroad system in 1970, and the "Q" ceased to exist. The C&S continued to operate the line until October 1986, when the Climax mine was all but closed because of decreased demand for molybdenite ore.

In spite of (and probably because of) all these problems, the South Park is loved by railfans because of the railroad's courage and determination to build and operate their line through some of the most spectacular scenery in Colorado. The route between Leadville and Climax is no exception.

The High Line route was sold to Stephanie and Kenneth Olsen in December 1987 to operate as a scenic railroad. Included in this sale were the right-of-way to Climax and the grade of the former Mineral Belt Railway that once served a number of mines in the Leadville Mining District. Also included were GP-9 diesel engines, #1714 and #1918, 5 cabooses, 4 boxcars, 8 flatcars, 1 hopper car, 1 flanger, the roadbed, 1800 tons of steel rail, 45,000 railroad ties, and roundhouse—all for $10! The Olsens purchased the depot, the city block on which the depot stands, and engine #641 from the City of Leadville.

After a frantic 5 months of converting flatcars to spacious excursion cars and refurbishing the roadbed and track, Colorado's newest railroad opened for business on Memorial Day, 1988.

HIGHWAYS TO LEADVILLE

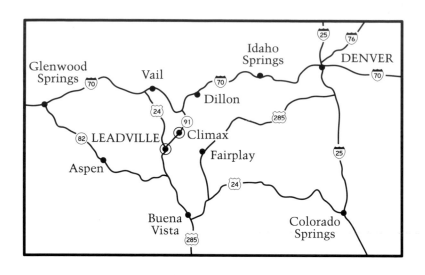

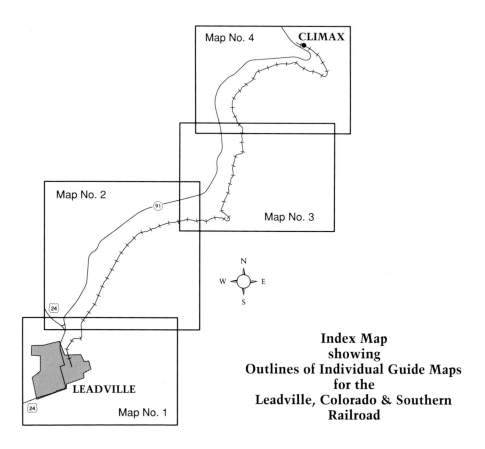

**Index Map
showing
Outlines of Individual Guide Maps
for the
Leadville, Colorado & Southern
Railroad**

MILE BY MILE GUIDE®

This Mile by Mile Guide is written so that points-of-interest, scenic highlights, historic locations, and geologic features are located using mileposts set along both sides of the track.

The mileposts are steel posts set about 6 to 12 feet from the track and have numbers visible from both directions. For convenience, the LC&S has also added narrow steel posts at each 1/2 mile, on the downhill side of the track. These posts have white bars painted on them. All mileposts are shown on the guide maps. The numbers on the mileposts indicate the distance by rail from Denver, where the Denver, South Park & Pacific Railroad started. Thus the Leadville depot is 151.2 miles by rail from Denver.

The terms *uphill* and *downhill* are used to locate points-of-interest along the track. Distant points-of-interest are described by compass direction.

SYMBOLS USED ON GUIDE MAPS

	LC&S track. Cross-ties are 1/10 mile apart
	Abandoned railroad grades.
	State Highway 91, other roads and streets
	Four-wheel-drive road.
	National forest boundary.
	County boundary.
	Rivers and streams.
	Marsh or swamp.
	Water tank
	Building
× 12,923'	Elevation along track or of mountain peak.
	Old mine or prospect.
	Glacial debris
	Tertiary igneous porphyry

Words in the glossary, p. 123, are in **bold**-face type the first time used in a chapter. Place names are capitalized in the guide the first time used.

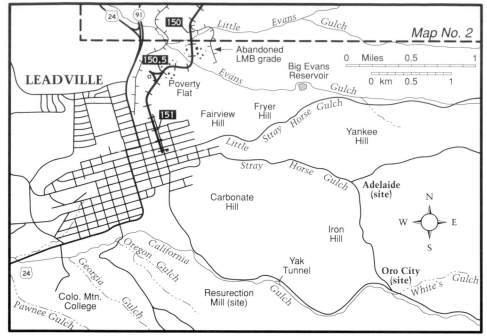

Mile
151.2 LEADVILLE, COLORADO & SOUTHERN RAILROAD DEPOT

The red brick depot, located at the corner of 7th and Hazel Streets, was completed in January 1893 during the Union Pacific Railroad (UP) ownership of the Denver, South Park & Pacific Railroad (DSP&P). It replaced a small frame passenger depot built soon after the (DSP&P) reached the Leadville in September 1884. The ground elevation at the depot is 10,208 ft.

From the depot, there are many magnificent views to the west, across the valley. From left to right are MT. ELBERT, el. 14,433 ft., the highest peak in Colorado, and MT. MASSIVE, el. 14,421 ft. To the northwest, the peak with the lower summit is GALENA MTN., 12,893 ft., and the higher one is HOMESTAKE PK., 13,209 ft. These two peaks are on the Continental Divide.

To the northeast is PROSPECT MTN., el. 12,614 ft. Many mines are on its southern slopes. Today's excursion winds along the northern slope of Prospect Mountain almost to the summit of FREMONT PASS and to the world's largest molybdenum mine at CLIMAX.

Southeast of the depot, the abandoned mine dumps on FRYER, FAIRVIEW, and CARBONATE HILLS stand out as huge piles of rubble above the houses. Visible on the eastern skyline from left to right are DYER MTN., el. 13,855 ft., MT. SHERMAN, 14,036 ft., MT. SHERIDAN, 13,748 ft., HORSESHOE MTN., 13,898 ft., and PTARMIGAN PK., 13,739 ft., all part of the Mosquito Range (map, inside front cover).

The old red DSP&P freight house, on the west side of the track just north of 8th Street, was built in 1884, along with a 32-foot-long Fairbanks scale, two-story section house, tool house, coal bin, stock pens and nine frame houses for railroad workers. By 1889 there were 12,840 feet of yard track; by 1897 an additional 1800 feet of track was in place. Only one storage track remains.

Every year Leadville hosts a 4-week celebration commemorating the mining camp, Oro City. On June 24, 1988, the Leadville, Colorado & Southern Railroad also took part in the celebration with the morning train being decorated with flags. Standing third from the left is Stephanie Olsen, co-owner of the LC&S. *(LC&S photo)*

Engine #1714 in front of the Leadville depot ready for the morning run to Climax. Sept. 16, 1988. *(Doris B. Osterwald)*

151.0 NORTH SIDE OF 11th STREET

The abandoned three-story red brick building on the west is St. Vincent's hospital. This second St. Vincent's was built in 1901 by the Sisters of Charity to replace their first hospital built in 1879 (photo, p 73). This building was used until 1954; a new St. Vincent's opened in 1958.

Miners were frequently hurt or killed in falls, fires, rockfalls, cave-ins and explosions during blasting. They were also prone to respiratory problems because of poor ventilation in the mines and the huge quantities of rock dust from the primitive drills ("widow makers") that did not use water to keep the dust down. Pneumonia and "miner's consumption" were common causes of death in the the early years before any sort of worker protection. St. Vincent's and other early hospitals were very important to all citizens of Leadville.

To the west, beyond St. Vincent's Hospital, and above the trailer court, is a nice view of TURQUOISE LAKE and SUGAR LOAF DAM. A small natural lake was enlarged to hold water diverted from the Fryingpan and Roaring Fork River basins, on the western slope. Water is brought to the eastern slope through the Charles H. Boustead tunnel to Turquoise Lake reservoir. The reservoir storage capacity is 129,400 acre-feet. From the lake, an extensive series of dams and conduits conveys the water to Colorado Springs, Pueblo, and other towns, farms, and reservoirs along the Arkansas River in eastern Colorado. Construction was completed in 1983 by the U.S. Bureau of Reclamation.

The flat sagebrush covered area east of the track is POVERTY FLAT. Beyond this flat to the southeast are the long abandoned headframes, hoist shacks, rotting mine buildings, and mine dumps on the brown, barren slopes of Fryer, Fairview and Carbonate Hills. These remaining relics offer stark evidence of Leadville's mining heritage. **VISITORS TO THE AREA SHOULD BE EXTREMELY CAUTIOUS AROUND THE MANY OPEN SHAFTS**.

The first silver discovery on Fryer Hill was made by George H. Fryer on April 4, 1878. When news of his strike, named the New Discovery, leaked out, many other would-be mining tycoons flocked to the area to search for their Eldorado. See p. 60 and p. 115 for more on the men who made Leadville famous with the discovery of the Little Pittsburg mine on Fryer Hill.

Along both sides of the track are large clumps of gray-green sagebrush and shrubby cinquefoil. Common wildflowers blooming during July and August include yellow butter and eggs, red to lavender fireweed, white yarrow and fall asters.

150.6 SPUR TRACK TO LC&S ROUNDHOUSE ON LEFT

The first track on the left is the former D&RG interchange track. Just beyond that track is the spur track to the LC&S roundhouse.

The roundhouse was originally an eight-stall building, covered with sheet-iron. By 1936 two stalls had been removed. After narrow gauge operations ceased in 1943, three more stalls were removed and the doors were enlarged to handle the larger standard gauge steam engines. The turntable was also removed at that time. After steam operations ceased in September 1962, the 50,000-gallon water tank was removed. Just beyond the track to the roundhouse is the south leg of the wye.

150.5   NORTH LEG OF WYE ON LEFT

Just beyond the north leg of the wye, the track crosses a gravel road which is the roadbed of a former D&RG branch, constructed in 1881 to reach mines on Fryer Hill. This branch was called EAST SPUR or FRYER HILL BRANCH. In 1898, the D&RG built 7-mile IBEX BRANCH to reach the ever-expanding mining district. In later years the D&RG converted the branch to standard gauge. It was used until 1941 when many mines closed during World War II.

150.25   CROSS EVANS GULCH

The track is built on **fill** above a small intermittent stream. To the east, the old grade of the D&RG Ibex Branch is visible as dark-gray to black fill above willows.

Track crosses the old OLATHE PLACER and then two lode claims, the BUSH and the OOLYTE. **Placer** claims are near-surface ore deposits formed by the concentration of mineral particles in loose debris. **Lode** claims are mining claims in ore deposits in consolidated rock.

To the east, many years ago, the Raymond, Sherman and McKay Smelter, Gage Hageman Smelter, Cummings & Finn Smelter and the Ohio & St. Louis Smelter were strung out along Evans Gulch. The Cummings & Finn Smelter was the largest and best known.

The last spike for the completion of the High Line was pounded into place along here on Feb. 5, 1884.

150.0   MILEPOST ON FILL AT LITTLE EVANS GULCH

The track is built on fill above the stream. Beyond the milepost, the track enters a lodgepole pine forest.

149.5   LODGEPOLE PINE FOREST

For the next 1/2-mile a straight section of track passes through a lodgepole pine forest. Lodgepole pines are easy to identify because of their thin, straight trunks and yellow-green needles. Much of this forest was logged off for use as buildings, mine timbers and in the manufacture of charcoal, needed in Leadville's smelters. Portions of the forest were also destroyed by fire during the 1870s and 1880s. The present forest is all second growth. Along with aspens, lodgepole pines are the first trees to sprout after a forest has been destroyed by fire or extensive logging.

Because these trees sprout at about the same time, they form dense forests in which little sunlight reaches the forest floor. These forests attract fewer animals and birds because of little growth on the ground. Low-growing kinnikinnik, dwarf junipers, and some aspens also grow along the track.

Many loose, rounded and smoothed boulders and cobbles are on each side of the track. These rocks (**glacial debris**, photo, p. 121) were carried in the ancient East Fork Glacier and were dumped in ridges and mounds of loose debris (**lateral moraines**) along both sides of the valley when the climate changed and the glaciers melted away.

Soon after DSP&P track reached Leadville in February 1884, the weather changed and throughout February and March severe blizzards brought all work to a

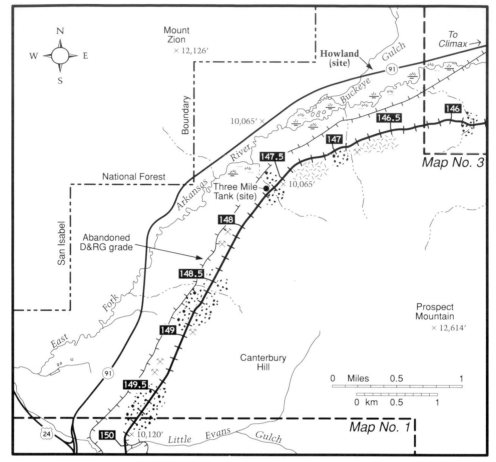

Map No. 2

halt. When the snow finally began to melt, crews found the roadbed was highly unstable where it was built on frozen glacial debris. Repairs and rebuilding continued throughout the summer. The line was finally opened for business Sept. 30, 1884.

Watch for miner's prospect holes along both sides of the track that were dug through glacial debris in attempts to reach mineralized **Paleozoic** and **igneous** rocks. Unfortunately, this area is north of the main mineralized zone and no bonanzas were found.

Milepost
149.0 MILEPOST IN ASPEN GROVE

Aspens reproduce from shallow roots which spread laterally. They send shoots upward to form a grove in which all the trees are related and are called "clones." The genetics of clone groves determine when the first leaves appear in the spring, when and to what color the leaves turn in the fall. Amounts of moisture, temperature and soil composition also affect these traits. Genetics also determine the shapes of the branches and the color of the bark, which varies from light gray-green to brownish-green to white. Bark of older aspens is whitish due to oxidation.

Red Indian paintbrush, tall yellow clumps of black-tipped senecios, golden asters, white yarrows and pearly everlastings, lavender fleabanes, lupines and raspberry shrubs bloom at different times in this area. A few tall spruce trees are scattered through the aspen groves. They survived fires and logging that destroyed most of the older forest. Spruce trees are easy to recognize because their cones hang downward from the tops of trees like pendants.

Between milepost 149.0 and 148.2 is the only portion of the route that is level. The grade between Leadville and Climax averages 1.6%, but varies from about 1.2 to 2.0%.

Milepost
148.5   GLACIAL DEBRIS ALONG TRACK

Beyond the milepost, the track comes out of the aspen forest and into an open area where the lovely, wide, U-shaped valley of the East Fork of the Arkansas River is visible for the first time. To the southwest is another glorious vista of MT. MASSIVE.

Milepost
148.0   MT. ZION IS THE PEAK ACROSS THE VALLEY

MT. ZION, el. 12,126 ft., is the rounded ridge directly across the valley. This peak is capped with highly faulted blocks of Middle Pennsylvanian Minturn Formation that has been **intruded** by **Tertiary** igneous rocks. Several avalanche tracks come down the steep slope to the valley floor.

The track crosses the former GOODSELL, THREE MILE and PROSPECT claims.

Mile
147.6   SITE OF THREE MILE WATER TANK

On the downhill side of the track, watch for the foundation of a former water tank. The original tank, built in 1884, burned (one wonders how that happened) and a new one was constructed in December 1907. The 50,000-gallon tank, fed by gravity from a spring above the track, was usually the first water stop for an eastbound freight train, although many of the standard gauge engines could make the French Gulch tank before needing water. Rotary snowplow trains would always take water here. The tank was removed in September 1962 after C&S engine 641 (on display at the depot) made its last run to Climax.

Milepost
147.5   MILEPOST IN MIXED FOREST

Along both sides of the track, interspersed with aspens and lodgepole pines, are some tall, slender Englemann and Colorado blue spruce trees that survived fires and logging. A key to identify these conifers is on p. 130.

Milepost
147.0   TRACK BUILT ON GLACIAL DEBRIS

A cut on the uphill side of the track exposes glacial debris. On the forest floor are low junipers, some willows, elderberry and rose shrubs.

Beyond the milepost, as the track winds back and forth around gentle curves, watch for the first glimpse of the high peaks of the Mosquito Range to the northeast. On the skyline (from left to right) is an unnamed peak that is south of Climax near the headwaters of the East Fork of the Arkansas River, and often called the

In February 1929, the Denver Water Board chartered a C&S train to study the entire route, as the Board hoped to build a dam in the Platte River Canyon. Such construction would force the abandonment of the railroad. Most photos were taken from the rear platform of the special. This view is just west of Three Mile water tank at M.P. 147.5.

The westbound Water Board Special has just passed the ice-incrusted Three Mile water tank near M.P. 147.5. The changes in the forest between 1929 and 1991 are quite dramatic. (Both photos, Colorado Railroad Museum)

SLEEPING INDIAN, el. 12,923 ft. Continuing to the right is MT. ARKANSAS, el. 13,795 ft, then the pyramid-shaped MT. TWETO, el. 12,682 ft. and the massive TREASUREVAULT MTN., el. 13,701 ft. More views will unfold as the train continues its steady climb toward the Continental Divide.

Mount Tweto was named in 1986 for Ogden Tweto, a well-known geologist who worked for the U. S. Geological Survey for more than 40 years and mapped much of the this region. He died in 1983.

Milepost
146.5 SITE OF HOWLAND AT BUCKEYE GULCH
BUCKEYE GULCH is directly across the valley. At the foot of the gulch (along State Highway 91) was HOWLAND, a small mining camp that probably provided supplies to the miners prospecting along the gulch and on the slope of Buckeye Peak. At one time perhaps 100 residents were living along this part of the valley. A Post Office operated from Aug. 8, 1879 until Sept. 19, 1882.

In 1935, when the price of gold was raised from $20 to $35 per ounce, another placer mining operation started in the gulch. Known as the HECTOR, it operated from June until October that year and intermittently during 1938 and possibly in 1939.

For the next mile, the grade of the former narrow gauge D&RG Blue River Extension may be seen through openings in the forest. The route crossed the valley floor from the lower side of Prospect Mountain to the highway opposite Birdseye Gulch (Maps 2 and 3). This branch was built in 1880 to reach the mining camps of Kokomo and Robinson in the Tenmile mining district and other camps along the Blue River. The track was completed from Leadville to Kokomo Dec. 27, 1880. The following year the line was extended to Wheeler Junction. The track was completed to Dillon and regular passenger service began Nov. 13, 1882.

Milepost
146.0 MILEPOST ON A CURVE
The dramatic scenery of the upper Arkansas River valley, the grade of the LC&S and the high peaks to the northeast come into view near this milepost.

Milepost
145.5 CROSS INDIANA GULCH
This steep gulch was originally called Elkhorn. It is not known when the name was changed to Indiana. During construction of the High Line in 1883-84, a trestle with ten 16-foot spans was built across the gulch. The original trestle was either removed or filled in during 1898. Sometime later, log cribbing (still visible below the track) was added to stabilize the roadbed. Surviving railroad documents indicate that just five trestles were built between Climax and Leadville. None remain to the present day.

Mile
145.3 SITE OF DYES SPUR
No information has been found on this siding, but railroad profiles and engineering drawings list this location as having a spur. It could not have been very long!

The Water Board Special has just gone around the curve at M.P. 146.5. The High Line above Birds Eye clearly shows, as does the abandoned D&RG Blue River Extension on the valley floor. Track was removed in 1924. The arrow indicates the location of a collapsed water tank.   *(Colorado Railroad Museum)*

This view, at M.P. 146, taken nearly 60 years after the Water Board Special traveled the High Line, also shows the railroad grade and majestic Mt. Arkansas on the skyline. The arrow points to the nearly horizontal line across the lower portion of the mountain, above treeline that is the trace of a major fault. Mt. Tweto, is to the right of Mt. Arkansas.   *(Frank W. Osterwald)*

On a sunny afternoon in 1887, DSP&P engine 217 stops at Indiana Gulch, M.P. 145.5 with a four-car freight train. Famous photographer, W. H. Jackson climbed a hill to capture this view looking east up the East Fork of the Arkansas River Valley. The trestle was removed in 1898. *(W. H. Jackson, Colo. Historical Society Collection)*

One hundred and one years later on Sept. 17, 1988, the vista remains very similar to that taken by Jackson. A paved highway has replaced a wagon road that once traversed the valley. *(Frank W. Osterwald)*

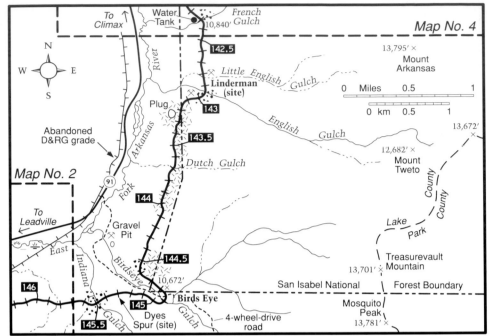

In this 1929 view, from the Water Board Special, the section house at Birds Eye is still standing. The train is at M.P. 144.8 just above the prospect in the Belden Formation mentioned in the text, p. 31. Close examination reveals the coaches are C&S business cars 910 and 911. The engine is probably #9, now owned by the Colorado Historical Society. (Colorado Railroad Museum)

145.0 MILEPOST IN A SMALL CUT IN GLACIAL DEBRIS

Have your camera ready as the train goes around BIRDS EYE CURVE, the sharpest of the entire trip. On the southeastern skyline, at the head of Birdseye Gulch, are TREASUREVAULT MTN. (left), el. 13,701 ft., and MOSQUITO PEAK, el. 13,781 ft. Farther to the right is an unnamed peak. All three peaks are part of the Mosquito Range.

Watch for a small abandoned mine dump across the valley a short distance below the track. This prospect was dug into dark-gray to black **sedimentary** rock of the middle Pennsylvanian Belden Formation.

144.95 CROSS BIRDSEYE CREEK

In 1884 a trestle with eight 16-foot spans bridged the creek. When the trestle was removed and replaced with a culvert and fill is not known, but it probably was prior to 1894 as the 1894 DL&G Bridge and Structure Book does not list a trestle at this location. Willows and sagebrush grow along both sides of the valley. (Note— USGS topographic maps show the name of the stream and small community at the foot of Birdseye Gulch as one word, but railroad timetables listed Birds Eye Station as two words.)

144.9 BIRDS EYE SECTION HOUSE SITE El. 10,672 ft.

A section house, tool house and a third structure were built on the east side of the gulch. A 532-foot spur track was located just below the buildings (photo, p. 107). The stone foundation of the section house is still visible. It is typical of early-day DSP&P stone mason's work. A small settlement of Birdseye was located in the valley at the mouth of Birdseye Gulch along the Arkansas River, where some placer mining was done.

A sawmill was located here at one time; many stumps remain on the slopes above the track. A lode mine in the area was worked during 1879 and a small stamp mill operated for a short time. A 4-wheel-drive road crosses the track and continues up the gulch to MOSQUITO PASS.

Much of the lower part of Birdseye Gulch is covered with glacial and landslide debris. The headwaters of Birdseye Gulch are on the west side of Mosquito Pass.

The name "Birdseye" supposedly was suggested by miners who thought the large-sized **feldspar** crystals **(phenocrysts)** in the Tertiary igneous **porphyry** resembled a bird's eye when the minerals sparkle in the sun. Because so many rich ore deposits were associated with the porphyries, miners called this rock "Mother of Gold." The phenocrysts of **orthoclase feldspar** cooled and solidified before the rest of the minerals in the rock crystallized so the feldspars grew to larger sizes than the minerals in the matrix of the rock. Porphyries are commonly found in **intrusive dikes**, **sills** and **stocks** and formed at shallow depths within the earth. Their mineral composition varies widely, and can be accurately identified and classified by looking at a thin section of the rock under a microscope.

Beyond the sharp curve at Birds Eye, outcrops of porphyry are visible on the uphill side of the track. The large-sized feldspar crystals (phenocrysts) are easy to spot on the rock surfaces. Many more chances to see this interesting rock will be found as the trip progresses.

The first train of the day, Sept. 16, 1988, rounds the 20° curve at Birds Eye with engine #1714 on the point (Doris B. Osterwald)

Close-up photo of orthoclase feldspar phenocrysts in porphyry. The specimen on the right illustrates the size to which the feldspar crystals may grow.

(Doris B. Osterwald)

144.8   SMALL PROSPECT HOLE ALONG TRACK

Watch for a 4x4 post on the uphill side of the track. It marks the location of a flange oiler installed by the C&S. Just beyond the post is a small cut in porphyry that is directly above a miner's prospect in the Belden Formation, about 75 feet below track level. The igneous porphyries acted as barriers to the ore-bearing fluids that were deposited <u>after</u> the porphyries were intruded into Paleozoic rocks. Perhaps a prospector started to dig here, in hopes of finding an ore deposit at the contact between the porphyry and Belden Formation. Apparently he soon gave up such exploration.

In later years, C&S section crews used this small opening to store tools; it sometimes had a canvas cover.

Several old telegraph poles, installed in 1884, still stand along the downhill side of the track.

144.5   MILEPOST NORTH OF BIRDSEYE GULCH

Across the valley are nice views of BUCKEYE PEAK, el. 12,867 ft. (Map, inside front cover) This peak consists of the Middle Pennsylvanian Minturn Formation that was intruded by Tertiary porphyries and broken by numerous **faults**.

Beyond this milepost, watch for the place where the D&RG grade crosses State Highway 91 opposite Birdseye Gulch and starts to climb along the lower slope of Buckeye Peak.

144.0   PORPHYRY ALONG BOTH SIDES OF TRACK

This is another place to see the porphyry and the large-sized orthoclase feldspar crystals (phenocrysts) that sparkle on the rock surfaces.

A garden of orange-colored lichens grow abundantly on the rock surfaces. Lichens are specialized plant-like organisms composed of a fungus and an alga, living so closely together (symbiotic association) that they appear to be one plant. They grow very slowly (1 mm to 10 mm in radius per year) on rocks, wood or soil and can survive long periods of drought and cold. Lichens vary in color from gray to green, olive, white, black, brown or orange and different species have many distinctive forms. They are very intolerant to air pollution and may become deformed, discolored or die when exposed to pollution from industrial plants or towns.

Wildflowers along the track are typical of the subalpine life zone. White yarrows and thistles, reddish paintbrushes and fireweed, yellow sulfur flowers, butter and eggs, black-tipped senecios, along with sagebrush, strawberries and raspberries thrive in this area. Redberried elder shrubs grow along the track. They have large clusters of small white flowers in June and July and by August have many small dark-red berries that are a favorite food of deer, elk, bears and birds.

143.7   CROSS DUTCH GULCH

According to an 1886 UP roster of bridges, buildings and structures, the longest trestle on the High Line was built here. This frame trestle had eleven 16-foot spans that stood 24 feet above the stream. Built in 1884, it was replaced in 1901 with a culvert and fill, as fill requires much less maintenance.

(Mileposts apparently were moved from time to time after the original ones were set in place by the DSP&P. Some of the present mileposts are at least 1/2 mile from where old records indicate they should be—especially along this stretch of the track.)

More steep outcrops of porphyry are on the uphill side of the track just beyond Dutch Gulch.

The COLORADO BELLE placer claim was along the stream channel.

Milepost
143.5 VIEWS OF MT. MASSIVE AND PROSPECT MTN. TO WEST

Mile
143.3 PORPHYRY PLUG ON LEFT
The rounded hill on the downhill side of the track is a mass of intrusive igneous porphyry that cooled and solidified in a vertical, pipe-like conduit. Such conduits are called **plugs**. Visible on the steep western side of the hill are a series of vertical, hexagonal-shaped columns (**columnar joints**) that formed as the result of contraction during cooling of the porphyry plug. This interesting structure is also easy to see from the bottom of the valley along the highway.

Milepost
143.0 SMALL CUT IN GLACIAL DEBRIS
This is another place to see jumbled boulders and cobbles, mixed with finer rock materials, so typical of the wide variety of debris found in a moraine.

On the eastern skyline is a closer view of Mt. Arkansas.

On the downhill side of the track, but not visible from the train, was a fairly large mine. The remains of an old industrial boiler lie near the mine dump.

Mile
142.95 CROSS ENGLISH GULCH ON A FILL
Along English Gulch were the LITTLE MARGARET, BISMARK, and LINCOLN lode claims. The headwaters of this stream are on the northern slope of Mt. Tweto (not visible from here). On the hillside are many stumps left from earlier logging. A private 4-wheel-drive road crosses the track and leads to some prospects.

Mile
142.9 SITE OF LINDERMAN El. 10,848 ft.
A 217-foot siding was located in this small cut on the straight section of track between English Gulch and Little English Gulch. No other data have been found about this siding.

Mile
142.8 CROSS LITTLE ENGLISH GULCH
Half buried in a small pond on the uphill side of the the track are the remains of an old boiler—all that is left from the LINCOLN LODE claim located east of the track. Much logging was done along here, and many mines and prospects were located on the upper slopes of Little English Gulch.

Beyond Little English Gulch the track crosses an open grass-covered slope.

Milepost
142.5 VIEW OF BUCKEYE PEAK El. 12,867 ft.
The steep, channel-like gullies that descend the east slope of Buckeye Peak are narrow corridors along which avalanches often roar down the slope during heavy winter snows. Vegetation is unable to grow to any height in these paths. Many such

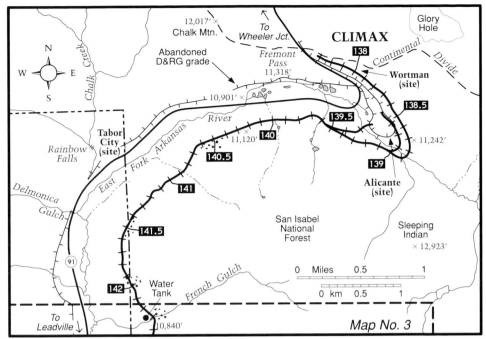

avalanche tracks are visible on the slopes of Buckeye Peak and Mt. Zion.

Mile
142.3 FRENCH GULCH WATER TANK El. 10,840 ft.
French Gulch heads on the northern slope of Mount Arkansas.

Having crossed Indiana, Dutch, English, Little English and now French Gulch, one can't help but wonder how and why those names came into being. No records have been found that explain the names or perhaps the competition that must have existed between small ethnic groups of miners working along these stream drainages.

The FRENCH GULCH, ADELINDE, LITTLE MARGARET, BISMARK, and INGERSOLL claims were located here at one time.

Milepost
142.0 MILEPOST ON OPEN, GRASS-COVERED HILLSIDE
Track leaves the huge old spruce forest and enters an open grassy area.

Cuts on the uphill side of the track expose more glacial debris. At this milepost, Buckeye Peak is visible from a slightly different perspective.

DSP&P records for 1885 (M.C.Poor, 1976, p. 449) show CLIFTON as a station with a 297-foot siding located at milepost 142.0, but no reference to such a station is found in the 1886 and 1894 UP roster of bridges, building and other structures.

Milepost
141.5 PANORAMIC VIEWS ACROSS THE VALLEY
Directly across the valley is DELMONICA GULCH, which descends from the eastern slope of Buckeye Peak. To the north is CHALK MOUNTAIN, el. 12,017 ft., on the Continental Divide. The building visible at the top of Chalk Mountain is part of a former high-altitude research facility.

35

Chalk Mountain is composed of a Tertiary **rhyolite** porphyry appropriately named the Chalk Mountain Rhyolite. The porphyry intrudes much older Minturn Formation.

Beyond the milepost and across the valley is CHALK CREEK GULCH. Chalk Creek flows into the Arkansas River here. Below the eroded cliffs at the lower end of the gulch, where a dirt road joins State Highway 91, is the site of TABOR CITY. This mining camp was named for Leadville's most illustrious citizen, H. A. W. Tabor.

During 1879 a town was laid out with streets numbered one through six and cross streets that were named Chestnut, Chalk, Main and Pine. Some cabins, several restaurants, two hotels, a blacksmith shop, livery stable and general store were built to serve travelers and miners. A Post Office opened April 14, 1879. By 1880 there were about 150 residents, but on Jan. 27, 1881 the Post Office was discontinued and by 1882 the "town" was abandoned.

Other names for the same general area include TABOR, TAYLOR CITY (named for a Colonel Taylor who purchased a site along Chalk Creek and also laid out a town), HALFWAY HOUSE and CHALK CREEK RANCH.

RAINBOW FALLS may be seen between the eroded cliffs above the site of Tabor City. Also visible on both sides of Rainbow Falls are traces of the D&RG grade. In order to gain altitude to reach the summit of Fremont Pass, the railroad built a trestle across Chalk Creek at Rainbow Falls. The structure was 175 feet long and 25 feet high. Just east of the trestle, the track went through a cut, which is still visible from the LC&S train.

Milepost
141.0 MILEPOST ON CURVE IN SPRUCE FOREST

Along both sides of the track many young spruce trees have grown since the High Line was converted to standard gauge in 1943. Much timber has been cut on the hillside above the track. Ground cover in this forest includes dwarf blueberry shrubs. Birds and mammals (including humans!) enjoy the sweet berries. In the fall, the tiny oval-shaped leaves turn a lovely golden-brown color.

Mile
140.85 SITE OF A TRESTLE

According to old records, a small trestle was built at this point in 1884. The wooden trestle had three 16-foot spans that were about 10 feet above the small intermittent stream located here. Nothing else is known of this structure or when it was replaced with a culvert and fill.

Milepost
140.5 FIRST VIEW OF CLIMAX MOLYBDENUM MINE

Mile
140.3 TALUS SLOPE El.11,120 ft.

This is as far as trains operates at present, due to the condition of the track. From this vantage point you can see the upper Arkansas valley and the headwaters of the Arkansas River, now a small mountain stream. Watch for marmots and pikas that live in the area. Also visible is the world's largest **molybdenum** mine at Climax.

BARTLETT MOUNTAIN, el. 13,555 ft., is on the skyline above the open pit of the Amax Company mine. The ancient glaciers that carved the U-shaped valley below the track, also gouged out a huge glacial **cirque** on the slope of Bartlett Mountain. Old photographs (pp. 44, 105, 142),taken many years before open pit mining began, offer graphic evidence of the erosive power of slowly moving ice. It is estimated that at least half of the 2 billion tons of molybdenite in the original deposit were removed as the cirque was gradually enlarged by glacial action.

Three separate inverted bowl-shaped ore bodies (stocks) of rhyolite porphyry, stacked one on top of another, were intruded into ancient **Precambrian metamorphic** and igneous rocks. These ore bodies were emplaced in four separate phases from middle Oligocene to earliest Miocene time—roughly 30 million years ago.

In 1879, prospector Charles J. Senter filed claims on a large outcrop of heavy, dark gray metallic-looking rock that appeared to contain large amounts of lead. Assays failed to reveal any lead and Charlie found he had no market for his unknown mineral deposit.

Finally in 1895 mineralogists at Colorado School of Mines identified the mineral in the rock as **molybdenite**. After metallurgists found a way to separate the complex ores containing molybenite, the first shipment of the strange new metal was made in 1915 by the American Metal Co. It was used to strengthen steel in weapons built during World War I. After the war, the mine closed because no other uses for the metal were known.

For the next 9 years the company struggled to survive. An extensive research and development program finally convinced automobile and steel companies that using molybdenum in steel made it much harder, tougher and more resistant to rust and corrosion. The company turned its first modest profit in 1929—just in time for the great depression. In 1957 the American Metal Company merged with the Climax Molybdenum Company to form Amax, Inc.

Open pit mining began in 1973 to supplement the underground operations. Peak production was in 1976 when the mine produced about 47,000 tons of ore per day with an average grade of 0.346 percent molybdenum disulfide. Between 1918 and March 1987, the mine produced 464.6 million tons of ore, yielding 1,892 billion pounds of molybdenum. Because of a world-wide drop in demand for molybdenum, production at Climax was drastically reduced, starting in 1982, and the mine closed in 1987. By mid- 1988 production had resumed and continues today.

In 1977 Amax built a large plant to treat water released into Tenmile Creek. The company also recycles the water used to carry the byproducts from milling operations to the tailing ponds north of Climax. Great care is taken to see that no heavy metals are released into Tenmile Creek, and trout now thrive in the stream. Reclamation and revegetation of the Glory Hole and the tailing ponds at such high elevations presents special problems, but the company continues its research and planning for complete restoration when mining at Climax ends.

Reserves are estimated to be at least 342 million tons of ore with a grade of 0.30 - 0.35 percent molybdenum disulfide. Life expectancy of the mine is 30 - 40 years. In 1948 a byproducts plant was built to recover tin, copper, and tungsten also.

Molybdenite is used in ferro-molybdenum alloys where hardness and toughness are needed. It is also used in electronic equipment, as a catalyst in the ink and dye industries, in lubricants and in the production of glass enamel.

Even though the train does not proceed past this point, notes are included to complete the history of the High Line to Climax.

View east toward Climax from M.P. 140.3 showing the large talus slope and the buildings at Amax Molybdenum Mine. From left to right are Bartlett Mtn, Clinton Peak, and Traver Peak are on the skyline.

The same view with a telephoto lens reveals the open-pit mine and the vast amount of rock that has been removed. The environmental consequences of mining must be balanced with the world's need for minerals. Amax Molybdenum Co. continues to make significant efforts to address these vital problems and has plans for reclamation once mining ceases. (Both photos, Doris B. Osterwald)

140.0 TRACK BUILT ON FILL ACROSS SMALL STREAM

Many willows are along both sides of the track.

139.5 MILEPOST AT SWITCH FOR TRACK TO STORKE CRUSHER OF CLIMAX MINE

The large pipes on the east side of the valley are covered conveyor belts that carry ore from the Storke crusher to the main mill at Fremont Pass.

139.0 MILEPOST AT SWITCH FOR TRACK TO STORKE PORTAL OF CLIMAX MINE

138.96 ALICANTE SECTION HOUSE SITE

The D&RG had a small station and 733 feet of side track at the town. There were also several hundred feet of snowsheds near the town. Several buildings and a Post Office were near the Alicante Mine, named for a city in Spain. Most of the "town" was along the D&RG track. The Post Office started June 15, 1881, but moved to Climax April 22, 1887. Other mines near Alicante included the JOHN REED, GOLD FIELD, WALTER SCOTT, and MINER'S COLLEGE. The Walter Scott had a 2,000-foot-long tram from the mine and a 20-stamp mill. The town, started in 1880, lasted until about 1888 and at its peak had perhaps 100 residents. The John Reed mine was noted for beautiful **rhodochrosite** crystals.

This photo, taken on a bright, sunny October afternoon, shows a portion of the beautiful cirque at the headwaters of the Arkansas River and Mt. Democrat on the skyline. In the foreground is the switchstand at M.P. 139.5, and the spur track to the Storke portal of the Climax mine. Portions of the spur have been dismantled by the BN.

(Ray W. Osterwald)

During the spring of 1899, scenes similar to this were all too common. The photo, taken just west of M.P. 142, raises more questions than it answers. The engine on this westbound train appears to be a DL&G 2-8-0, and the square shape of a rotary snowplow hood is visible to the right of the crewman. The derailed engine is a D&RG C-16 that was headed east before it left the track and appears to have lain here for some time. Perhaps the Blue River Extension was already blocked and the D&RG was trying to reach Dillon on the DL&G route. Unfortunately, the details surrounding this photo have been lost in time.

(Colorado Railroad Museum)

Above the track, on the southern skyline, is the northernmost ridge of Mount Arkansas. This unnamed peak, el. 12,923 ft., is often referred to as the SLEEPING INDIAN, which is, from this location, a very apt name.

Mile
138.85 TRACK CROSSES ARKANSAS RIVER
This is the site of the fifth trestle built on the High Line. A wooden, trestle with five 6-foot spans was built in 1883. When it was removed is not known.

From this point is a majestic view southeastward toward MT. DEMOCRAT, el. 14,148 ft., on the skyline. The huge bowl below the mountain is another glacial cirque. The floor of the cirque is a rich **wetland** on which willows and many subalpine and alpine wildflowers bloom during July and August.

Mile
138.06 WORTMAN MINE El. 11,240 ft.
A four-car spur connected with the Wortman mine, started by G. C. Wortman, whose mine was near the the John Reed mine. Some high-grade ore was produced, but the mine closed in the late 1880s. A Post Office served the area from Sept. 25, 1900 to Aug. 31, 1908 and again from May 25, 1916 to Jan. 15, 1919.

Mile
137.46 CLIMAX, AT SUMMIT OF FREMONT PASS El. 11,318 ft.
Even though the D&RG crossed Fremont Pass in 1880, no station or facilities were built at the summit until mining started at the Climax mine. In 1884, when the DSP&P finally reached the top of Fremont Pass, they built a covered turntable and other facilities and named the station Climax. Rails of the two companies were the minimum distance apart, and yet there was no interchange track! After all, these two railroads were in fierce competition with each other.

DSP&P records for 1889-97 list a turntable, coaling facility, telegraph office, bunk house, and 38-car siding. An engineering drawing of facilities at Climax (on file at the Colorado Railroad Museum in Golden), and traced from an October 1885 survey, shows a 50-foot covered turntable attached to an engine house. Total length of the building was 140 feet. Some records indicate that the engine house burned in 1907, but a 1909 C&S drawing shows the building in place.

Fremont Pass was named for explorer Lt. John C. Fremont, who wandered through much of Colorado on several expeditions searching for a suitable railroad route across the Continental Divide. Even though both the D&RG and DSP&P finally conquered Fremont Pass, Lt. Fremont never crossed it.

Water in the Arkansas River eventually reaches the Mississippi River and flows into the Gulf of Mexico, whereas water on the eastern side of the divide in Tenmile Creek flows into the Colorado River on its long journey to the Pacific Ocean.

A DSP&P passenger train on the left, and a D&RG mixed train posed for W. H. Jackson in this famous view looking east toward the headwaters of the Arkansas River. Mt. Democrat is on the skyline to the left and the northern flank of Mt. Arkansas is on the right. This mountain is locally referred to as the Sleeping Indian. The photo, probably taken in 1887, shows both tracks that wind around the valley, crossing the river on timbered trestles. The mining town of Alicante is in the valley along the D&RG track and snowsheds. *(Colorado Historical Society)*

On a cold day in February 1929, the Denver Water Board Special stopped just west of M.P. 139, long before the spur track to the Storke portal of the Climax mine was built, and many years after Alicante was abandoned *(Colorado Railroad Museum)*

Famous railroad photographer Otto C. Perry rode in the caboose of an eastbound doubleheaded freight on June 16, 1943. Engines #76 and #74 are just rounding the curve at M.P. 139 and approaching the trestle across the Arkansas River.
(Denver Public Library, Western History Dept.)

On Feb. 22, 1962, railroad author and photographer, Dick Kindig, found the fireman shoveling coal forward in the tender, as engine #641 approaches Climax at 12:39 p.m. with a 5-car freight. The Storke portal and the crusher plant for the Amax mine are located near where Alicante once stood. The large pipes that ascend the hill cover conveyor belts that carry crushed ore to the mill for refining. *(Richard D. Kindig)*

The Denver Water Board Special arrived at Climax from Dillon on a cloudy, cold day in February 1929. The buildings visible in the cirque include dorms, a boarding house and dining room for the miners.   (Colorado Railroad Museum)

In 1935 or 1936, Climax had grown significantly when Otto Roach of Denver was commissioned to take this panorama. Enlarged portions of the photo are on p. 105.
(Photo courtesy, Climax Molybdenum Co.)

RETURN TRIP TO LEADVILLE

Mile
140.3 TALUS SLOPE

On both sides of the track is a large **talus** slope. These loose blocks of Precambrian **granite** and **diorite** have broken off outcrops high on the hillside above the track and come to rest in a position of equilibrium on the slope surface. Many gray-green lichens grow on these loose rocks.

Marmots and pikas like to live on such rocky slopes. Maybe you will be lucky and see one of these interesting mammals.

Milepost
141.0 MILEPOST IN SPRUCE FOREST

Notice how the cones of the Engelmann spruce and blue spruce trees hang down like pendants from the tops of the trees.

Mile
141.5 RAINBOW FALLS ACROSS VALLEY AT CHALK CREEK

If you missed seeing these falls on the way up, watch for them on the return trip between mileposts 141.5 and 142.0. Watch for a dirt road that leaves the main highway and climbs along Chalk Creek Gulch. Rainbow Falls are visible in the eroded cliffs above and to the left of that road.

During the terrible winter of 1898-99 both the D&RG and DSP&P (then the DL&G) tracks were closed by repeated snowslides and a host of other problems. During the spring of 1899 photographers had a chance to film D&RG rotary snowplow No. 2 as it carefully crossed the trestle at Rainbow Falls (photos, pp. 50, 51).

Milepost
142.0 MILEPOST ON OPEN, GRASS-COVERED SLOPE

Much timber was cut on the hillsides of this area. There is a nice view down the valley in which the Arkansas River meanders back and forth.

Mile
142.3 FRENCH GULCH WATER TANK

The vegetation here is different from that found around Leadville and is typical of that found in the upper subalpine life zone. Summer wildflowers include yellow alpine paintbrushes, sulfur flowers, black-tipped senecios, golden asters, avens, several species of buckwheat, little red elephants, kings crowns, rose crowns, lavender lupines, harebells, purple fringes, columbines, and tiny fleabanes.

Common mammals in the area include marmots, pikas, deer, elk, chipmunks, golden-mantled ground squirrels, and sometimes Nuttall's cottontails and snowshoe hares. The summit of Mt. Elbert (left) and Mt. Massive (right) are on the western skyline to the right of Prospect Mountain. Many more glimpses of these peaks will unfold as the train continues toward Leadville.

The 47,500-gallon wooden tank has had an interesting history. The tank originally stood on the opposite side of the track, but in 1943 when the High Line was converted to standard gauge, it was moved and raised so the spout would fit over the taller standard gauge engine tenders. Water for the tank came from a small reservoir on the hill above the track.

Aug. 25, 1943 was the last day of narrow gauge operations on the High Line. In this photo, #76, uncoupled from its train, stopped for water at French Gulch tank, while workers prepared to move the tank to the opposite side of the track. This was necessary so the spout would fit over the larger standard gauge steam engines.
(Burlington Northern Railroad photograph. Hol Wagner collection)

French Gulch water tank on a beautiful fall day in 1988.   *(Doris B. Osterwald)*

The following photographs document a derailment at French Gulch June 23, 1980. A heavy rainstorm filled the small reservoir above the track and the overflow washed out the dam. The afternoon freight left Climax at 3:30 p.m. with BN diesel engine #6223, 10 cars, and a caboose. When engineer Colin Bills and fireman W. A. King saw the washout, Colin put his brake valve into emergency and the men jumped from the cab. Neither were hurt, but the engine dropped into the gulch and one tank car tottered over the edge of the washout. (Color photos, LC&S collection)

The Leadville Herald Democrat reported it would cost at least $50,000 for culvert and track repair, $45,000 to pull the engine out of the gulch and at least $20,000 for engine repairs. A replacement engine, #6220 arrived in Leadville to help with recovery operations. June 28, 1980.

To add insult to injury, when the damaged engine was returned to Leadville for repairs, it was found the pit in the roundhouse was not deep enough to drain the fuel oil from the tank, so it was shoved onto the wye to drain the oil. In trying to couple the two engines together, #6220 shoved #6223 too hard and it rolled forward and off the end of the wye because the brakes would not work! A crane was dispatched from Denver to rescue the engine. July 5, 1980. *(Both photos, Ed Fulcomer)*

Golden aster, Solidago spathulata

Macronema discoideum
(This species needs a common name.
Any suggestions?)

Black-tipped senecio, Senecio atratus
and tiny blue erigerons.

The winter of 1898-99 was one of the worst on record in Colorado and railroads were blocked for weeks at a time. Finally in April, a D&RG snowplow extra with rotary #2 started east toward Dillon. Photographers were invited along, and took the photo above and those on the following page. These historic pictures were made as the rotary, pushed by engine #419 and two others, paused at Rainbow Falls trestle over Chalk Creek.

(Unknown photographer. From an album in the Johnson Collection, copied April 6, 1968 by Jackson Thode, through the courtesy of R. O. Williams.)

Top right: It is likely that one of the men standing ahead of the train took the photo above as they are using cameras. The consist of the train is clearly visible—along with the amount of work remaining to plow through the cut east of the trestle.

(Colorado Railroad Museum)

Bottom right: This action photo was taken as the plow train, pushed by three hardworking Baldwin engines, climbs toward Climax. Traver Peak is on the skyline above the plume of snow tossed out by the rotary. Coach 455 had an interesting 57 years on the D&RG narrow gauge. Built in 1883 or 1884 as an "emigrant sleeper," it was rebuilt in April, 1889 after being damaged in a derailment. In October 1910, it was rebuilt into the second parlor car "Durango," as the first was destroyed in a wreck on the Silverton Branch in 1910. In 1937 the coach was again remodled and renamed the "Gunnison." In 1942 it was sold to the National Railways of Mexico. (Colorado Railroad Museum)

The INGERSOLL PLACER was located along here. During construction of the High Line, owners of the claim erected a barricade to prevent DSP&P crews from building across their property. Farther west between English Gulch and Dutch Gulch, the owners of the OLD CROWN claim also filed an injunction to keep the railroad off their property. Both properties had faulty titles, however, and the injunctions and barricades caused little delay in spiking down track.

Milepost
142.5 VIEW OF PROSPECT MOUNTAIN TO SOUTHWEST

Mile
142.8 CROSS LITTLE ENGLISH GULCH
Perhaps you missed seeing the remains of an old boiler half buried in a small pond below the track on on the uphill side. If so, now is a good time for another view of this relic. Prospects were located along all the streams that flow into the East Fork of the Arkansas River.

Mile
142.95 CROSS ENGLISH GULCH

Milepost
143.0 SMALL CUT IN GLACIAL DEBRIS
This is one of several locations to see the wide variety of rock material that has been deposited along both sides of the valley by glaciers that once flowed down the East Fork of the Arkansas River Valley.

The afternoon train on its return trip to Leadville just west of English Gulch at M.P. 143.25. Sept. 17, 1988. *(Frank W. Osterwald)*

About 9 weeks before the end of narrow gauge operations on the High Line, Otto Perry found #74 westbound at Dutch Gulch, M.P. 143.7, with 10 cars of freight. June 16, 1943. (Otto C. Perry, Denver Public Library, Western History Dept.)

Mile
143.3 PORPHYRY PLUG
Watch on the downhill side, as the train goes through a cut, for another view of this interesting geologic feature. From here to milepost 145.5 are the best places to see the outcrops along the uphill side of the track of Tertiary igneous porphyry with large orthoclase phenocrysts that are visible on the outcrops.

Milepost
143.5 VIEW OF MT. MASSIVE AND PROSPECT MOUNTAIN

Mile
143.7 CROSS DUTCH GULCH
No evidence remains of a wooden trestle that once bridged this stream.

Milepost
144.0 VIEW OF D&RG GRADE IN VALLEY
If you missed seeing traces of the old D&RG grade that crossed the floor of the valley, there are many good viewpoints along here. Directly across the valley, where the highway makes a curve to the north, is the point where the grade began to climb along the eastern slope of Buckeye Peak. No trains ran on this branch after February 1911 and rails were finally removed in 1924.

Mile
144.95 BIRDSEYE GULCH
Have your camera ready for photos of the train as it curves around the head of Birdseye Gulch on the only 20° curve on the High Line. Treasurevault Mountain and Mosquito Peak are on the eastern skyline.

145.0 MILEPOST AT SMALL CUT IN GLACIAL DEBRIS

145.5 CROSS INDIANA GULCH

On the downhill side of the track, watch for log cribbing that has been added to stabilize the roadbed. Surviving records do not indicate when this cribbing was installed, but old photographs taken during the 1940s show the cribbing in place.

Milepost

146.0 MILEPOST ON CURVE

Deer, rabbits and even coyotes have been spotted in the timber near the track. Wildflowers include several species of yellow composites and clover, lavender lupine, fleabane, and thistles. Many tall blue spruce trees, the Colorado State tree, thrive on these moist north-facing slopes.

Milepost

146.5 SITE OF HOWLAND AT BUCKEYE GULCH

Between openings in the forest near the milepost are more opportunities to see the site of the old mining camp of Howland at the foot of Buckeye Gulch, and the old D&RG grade in the middle of the valley, on the south side of the Arkansas River.

Milepost

147.5 MILEPOST IN MIXED FOREST

For the next 2 miles the track winds through a forest of aspen, lodgepole pine, some Engelmann spruce, and Colorado blue spruce. Notice the variety of wildflowers and shrubs growing on the forest floor, including dwarf junipers, willows and kinnikinnik. Kinnikinnik is a small shrub with glossy evergreen leaves and brown woody stems. In the early summer the plant has tiny, pink urn-shaped flowers and by fall has bright dark-red berries that are a favorite food for wildlife. Kinnikinnik thrives on poor and rocky soils.

As the train continues toward Leadville, watch for changes in the amount of vegetation growing on the forest floor.

Mile

147.6 SITE OF THREE MILE WATER TANK JUST BEYOND SMALL STREAM

The foundation for the water tank is on the downhill side in a grove of aspen trees.

Milepost

148.0 VIEW OF GEOLOGIC SILL ACROSS VALLEY

On the lower slope of Mt. Zion, directly across the valley and several hundred feet above the highway, is a light-colored outcrop of flat-lying rocks. An igneous porphyry was intruded between layers of older sedimentary rocks to form a sill. Below the porphyry sill is a layer of Cambrian Sawatch **Quartzite** and lying above the sill is Ordovician Manitou **Dolomite** (photo, p. 121).

Milepost

148.5 LATERAL MORAINE ACROSS VALLEY

Between openings in the forest are nice views of Mt. Massive and the Arkansas River valley below. To the west and southwest, the low, tree-covered ridges on both sides of the valley are lateral moraines deposited by the East Fork

An eastbound freight, doubleheaded with engines #76 and #74, makes a water stop at Three Mile tank. The #76 has finished at the spout, and the engineer is moving the train ahead so #74 can have its turn. Narrow gauge operations are almost over, as the standard gauge rails are in place. June 16, 1943.
(Otto C. Perry, Denver Public Library, Western History Dept.)

Glacier. The debris in such moraines are rock fragments plucked from the valley walls upstream and carried in the ice to this lower elevation (photo, p. 121).

Milepost
149.0 MILEPOST IN ASPEN GROVE
Old telegraph poles still stand on the downhill side of the track. At several places the wires remain.

As the train continues toward Leadville, the track enters a forest that is predominantly lodgepole pine. This forest sprouted after a forest fire in the 1870s. Fires open the forests, remove the underbrush, and leave bare soils on which lodgepole pine seeds can easily sprout in full sunlight. Lodgepole cones, if not destroyed by fire, open up and release their seeds when heated to temperatures between 113°F and 122°F. The seeds are then spread by birds and mammals.

Milepost
149.5 LODGEPOLE PINE FOREST
Vegetation on the ground is sparse because relatively little sunlight can penetrate the forest canopy.

Not visible from the train, but directly below the track on the southeastern side of Prospect Mtn. and below Colorado Highway 91, is the portal of the Leadville Drainage Tunnel built in 1943 to drain water from mines east of Leadville. At present [1991] a treatment plant is being constructed by the EPA to remove all heavy metals from the water coming from the tunnel. This tunnel is near the earlier Canterbury Tunnel, which was never very successful, but is providing some water to the City of Leadville.

View south at M.P. 149.9 where the grade of the former Leadville Mineral Belt Railway (LMB) connected with the mainline of the DL&G. August 19, 1990.

(Doris B. Osterwald)

Mile
149.85 HIGH VOLTAGE POWER LINES CROSS TRACK

Less than 1/10 mile beyond the power lines, on the uphill side of the track, an old railroad grade goes eastward through a cut in the timber.

Mile
149.9 FORMER LEADVILLE MINERAL BELT RAILWAY GRADE

On the uphill side of the train is a small cut that curves eastward from the track. This is the point where the Leadville Mineral Belt Railway (LMB) branched off the main line. It was built in 1898 to serve some of the famous mines on Fryer Hill and in the Graham Park area (map, pp. 58-59). In June 1900, the LMB was sold to the C&S for $15,377.23. At one time there was a siding to hold loaded and empty gondola cars.

The LMB was built with a standard gauge third rail, and the railroad interchanged with both the CM and D&RG. Narrow gauge cars of ore concentrates left Leadville on the C&S, while standard gauge cars left Leadville on the CM or D&RG. The C&S operated this 3.09-mile branch until 1937. In 1938 the company was granted permission to abandon all its narrow gauge routes, except the High Line between Climax and Leadville.

Milepost
150.0 MILEPOST ON FILL AT LITTLE EVANS GULCH

Milepost
150.5 NORTH LEG OF WYE ON RIGHT

Just beyond the wye, the track crosses a gravel road which is the roadbed of

The road crossing at M.P. 150.5 is the abandoned grade of the D&RG branch to the Chrysolite, Ibex and other mines east of Leadville. This is where the D&RG parked an engine in 1883 to block DSP&P construction crews building east from Leadville.

(Ray W. Osterwald)

a former D&RG branch line that served the mines east of Leadville. This is the location of the infamous crossover where in August or September 1883 the D&RG parked a live locomotive on their track in an attempt to prevent DSP&P crews from building into Leadville (p. 12).

Milepost
151.0 ON NORTH SIDE OF 11th STREET

Mile
151.2 LEADVILLE, COLORADO & SOUTHERN RAILROAD DEPOT

Without the intrepid prospectors who combed the hills for their hidden treasures, or the miners who tore the ore from rock with their bare hands, the beloved DSP&P and other railroads would never have been built to Leadville or to any of the other famous mining centers. The businessmen, promoters and entrepreneurs who built the DSP&P, D&RG and CM all had one goal in mind—make money carrying men and machinery to the mining camps and carry ore to eastern markets. The rise and fall of these railroads is outlined in the Timeline, p. 60.

Part of the extensive railroad network that served Leadville was a dual gauge track that the C&S built in 1900 southward from the present station to the Bon Air Mine (mine No. 8 pp. 58-59). The track also connected with the CM and D&RG at the southern end of Leadville. This track was removed in 1937. Little evidence of the location of that branch remains. Thanks for riding on the LC&S. We hope that you enjoyed your excursion and the trip back in history to the time when railroads were the main form of transportation through the Colorado mountains, and we look forward to your next visit.

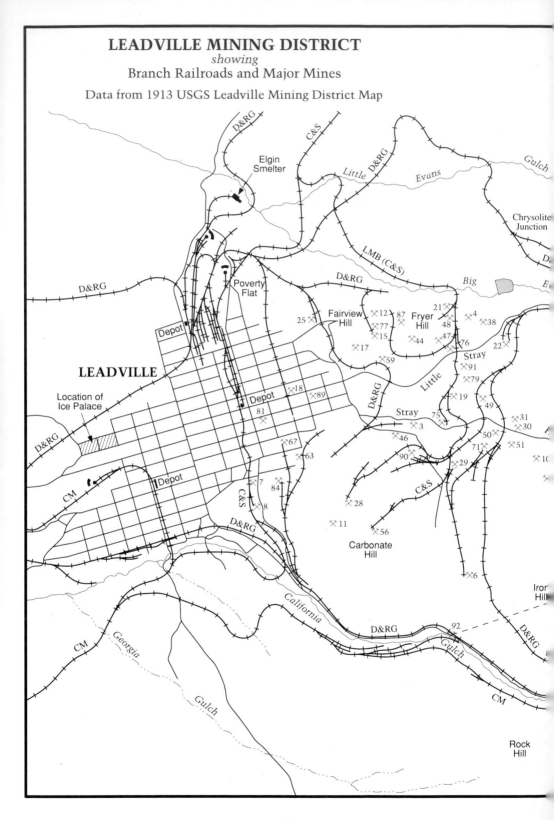

LEADVILLE MINING DISTRICT
showing
Branch Railroads and Major Mines
Data from 1913 USGS Leadville Mining District Map

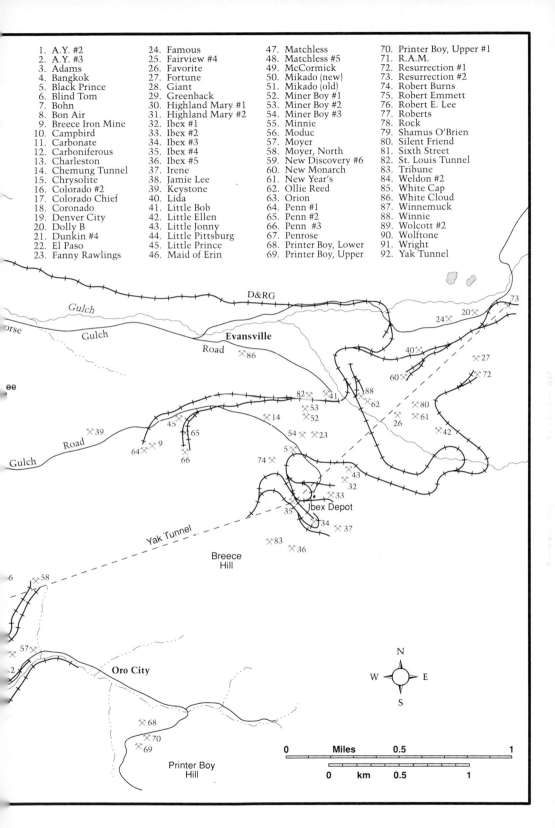

1. A.Y. #2	24. Famous	47. Matchless	70. Printer Boy, Upper #1
2. A.Y. #3	25. Fairview #4	48. Matchless #5	71. R.A.M.
3. Adams	26. Favorite	49. McCormick	72. Resurrection #1
4. Bangkok	27. Fortune	50. Mikado (new)	73. Resurrection #2
5. Black Prince	28. Giant	51. Mikado (old)	74. Robert Burns
6. Blind Tom	29. Greenback	52. Miner Boy #1	75. Robert Emmett
7. Bohn	30. Highland Mary #1	53. Miner Boy #2	76. Robert E. Lee
8. Bon Air	31. Highland Mary #2	54. Miner Boy #3	77. Roberts
9. Breece Iron Mine	32. Ibex #1	55. Minnie	78. Rock
10. Campbird	33. Ibex #2	56. Moduc	79. Shamus O'Brien
11. Carbonate	34. Ibex #3	57. Moyer	80. Silent Friend
12. Carboniferous	35. Ibex #4	58. Moyer, North	81. Sixth Street
13. Charleston	36. Ibex #5	59. New Discovery #6	82. St. Louis Tunnel
14. Chemung Tunnel	37. Irene	60. New Monarch	83. Tribune
15. Chrysolite	38. Jamie Lee	61. New Year's	84. Weldon #2
16. Colorado #2	39. Keystone	62. Ollie Reed	85. White Cap
17. Colorado Chief	40. Lida	63. Orion	86. White Cloud
18. Coronado	41. Little Bob	64. Penn #1	87. Winnemuck
19. Denver City	42. Little Ellen	65. Penn #2	88. Winnie
20. Dolly B	43. Little Jonny	66. Penn #3	89. Wolcott #2
21. Dunkin #4	44. Little Pittsburg	67. Penrose	90. Wolftone
22. El Paso	45. Little Prince	68. Printer Boy, Lower	91. Wright
23. Fanny Rawlings	46. Maid of Erin	69. Printer Boy, Upper	92. Yak Tunnel

TIMELINE
for
LEADVILLE and RAILROAD HISTORY

THE OLD ROUTE TO LEADVILLE.

YEAR	LEADVILLE and COLORADO HISTORY	RAILROAD HISTORY
1854	• First signs of placer gold found below Leadville along a stream called Cache Creek near what later became the town of Granite (located south of Leadville). The creek was named by a group of miners who were forced to "cache" their supplies over the winter.	
1858	• First report of placer gold in Dry Creek near present-day Denver.	
1859	• Placer gold found by George A. Jackson on Jan. 7 in the mountains west of Denver at the junction of Chicago Creek and Clear Creek. • John H. Gregory found placer gold in March in a gulch now called Gregory. • W. G. Russell found gold below the Gregory claim in September. • First stream quartz mill was built near the Gregory claim in September. • A. G. Kelley found placer gold near present-day town of Granite. • Late in the season, Slater and Company discovered gold at the junction of the Arkansas River and what became California Gulch. The gold rush to Colorado was on!	
1860	• Prospectors flocked to Clear Creek and surrounding gulches, and new strikes were made throughout the year. • Kelley returned in March to his claim and found other prospectors already at work along the Arkansas River and tributary streams. His claim became known as "Kelley's Bar" or the "Kelley Mining District." • The first rich strike was in April in a gulch named California because Abe Lee, a prospector who had been in California during the 1849 gold rush said: "I've just got California in this here pan." • Placer mining was difficult, however, because of large quantities of heavy	

YEAR	LEADVILLE and COLORADO HISTORY	RAILROAD HISTORY
1860 cont.	black sands which were later identified as rich silver-lead ores. • The first permanent settlement, Oro City, was a few crude cabins strung out along both sides of California Gulch (photo, p 65). • Horace Tabor, his wife, Augusta, and their young son arrived in California Gulch in May. Because Augusta was the first woman in the new community, miners built her a cabin in two days time. Augusta was soon busy feeding hungry men and often was called upon to nurse the injured and sick. Horace panned for gold and recovered between $5,000 and $7,000 the first season. • By midsummer claims were also located in nearby Iowa Gulch and the population grew rapidly. Mining was done by sluices, long toms, hand rockers and pans.	 MINER AND CRADLE.
1861	• Post Office was established Feb. 16 at Oro City, Kansas Territory. • Colorado became Colorado Territory Feb. 28. Capital was in Golden. • Lake County was one of 17 original counties in Colorado Territory and Oro City was the first county seat for Lake County. • Civil War started Apr. 12. Many miners returned home to fight. • First ditch built to bring water from Evans Gulch to California Gulch to wash gold from the gravels. • Tabors used their profits to buy supplies and opened a store at Oro City. Augusta ran the store while Horace continued prospecting.	 THE FLUME.
1862	• Because California Gulch appeared to have been worked out, Tabors moved their store to Buckskin Joe, the newest mining camp in South Park, located west of Alma.	

YEAR	LEADVILLE and COLORADO HISTORY	RAILROAD HISTORY
1862 cont.	• A flume was built in Cache Creek Gulch to bring additional water needed to wash the placer gold from the deep, narrow gulch.	
1864	• First silver strike in Colorado was on McClellan Mountain about 5 miles southwest of Georgetown. • The mining towns of Central City, Black Hawk, Eureka, Empire City and Nevadaville continued to grow.	
1865	• Lake County seat moved from Oro City to Twin Lakes because of decreased mining activity during the Civil War. • First smelter in Colorado was built at Black Hawk.	• First railroad chartered in Colorado was the Colorado and Clear Creek Railroad (C&CC) to be built from Golden up Clear Creek to the mining camps. The next year the name was changed to Colorado Central and Pacific Railroad (CC&P). This railroad was financed by Golden interests, including W.A.H. Loveland.
1867	• Charles Mater settled at Granite and opened the first general store. He later moved his business to Leadville. • Boston & Colorado Smelter built at Black Hawk in June. • Capital of Colorado Territory moved from Golden to Denver. • Estimates of production from the placers in Lake County between 1859 and 1867 are $5,272,000 in gold and $50,422 in silver.	• Union Pacific (UP) track crossed the northeastern corner of Colorado near present-day Julesburg. • Ground was broken in May for the CC&P to connect Golden and Denver. In June the company was reorganized and refinanced with UP backing. • The Denver Pacific Railway & Telegraph Co. (DP) was organized in November to connect Denver with the UP at Cheyenne, Wyoming.
1868	• In June the first gold lode deposit, The Printer Boy (Nos. 68, 69[†]), was discovered above Oro City by miners Cooper Smith and Charles J. Mullen. The Printer Boy closed some years later because of water seeping into the mine, a continuing problem for most Leadville mines. • First stamp mill in the district was built at the Printer Boy Mine to crush rock and ore.	• No track was laid in Colorado during the year, but 6 miles of grading for the CC&P was done between Golden and Denver. • Ground was broken in Denver May 13 for the DP to connect Denver with Cheyenne.

[†]Numbers following the name of a mine locate that mine on the Leadville Mining District map, pp. 58-59.

YEAR	LEADVILLE and COLORADO HISTORY	RAILROAD HISTORY
1868 cont.	• Tabors returned to Oro City and opened a general store. Horace was appointed postmaster and express agent and continued to grubstake miners. Augusta went back to cooking and running the store. • Oro City moved farther up California Gulch and became known as Oro No. 2 or New Oro City. • Lake County seat moved to Granite. • Total Lake County production of gold was $60,000 and $600 in silver.	
1869	• Total mineral production in Lake County was $90,000 in gold and and $900 in silver.	• The first transcontinental railroad (UP) was completed May 10 at Promontory Point, Utah. • The Colorado Central & Pacific Railroad's name was changed to the Colorado Central Railroad Co. (CC) Jan. 26. • DP track reached Evans, Colo., in December.
1870	• Mineral production was still disappointing for Lake County as only $65,000 in gold and $618 in silver were reported. 	• The first passenger train to reach Denver arrived June 22 on the DP. It was built with financial assistance of the Kansas Pacific Railroad (KP) which was building westward from Kansas City, Mo., to Denver via Cheyenne Wells, Kit Carson, Hugo, and Strasburg. • KP track reached Denver Aug. 15. • Both KP and CC were interested in gaining control of any railroads built into the mountains. • The Denver & Rio Grande Railway Co. (D&RG) was chartered Oct. 27 to build southward from Denver to Mexico City and westward into the mining regions of Colorado. This was the first narrow gauge railroad in the State. • The first CC train left Golden and arrived in Denver on Sept. 24, via DP track.

View east of Oro City, probably in the early 1870s. Printer Boy Hill is on the right. (Colorado Mountain History Collection)

YEAR	LEADVILLE and COLORADO HISTORY	RAILROAD HISTORY
1871	• In addition to the Printer Boy, active mines were the Five Twenty, Pilot, American Flag and Berry Tunnel. • Gold production amounted to $100,000 and silver was only $1,534. • During the winter of 1871-72, it snowed for 62 days and the cabins at the Printer Boy Mine were completely buried in snow.	• D&RG track-laying was completed to Colorado Springs in October, but regular train service did not start until Jan. 1, 1872. Severe early winter weather prevented the necessary ballast and surfacing work to be completed.
1872	• Granite was almost deserted as placer claims along Cache Creek were nearly played out. • Twin Lakes began attracting tourists. • A large encampment of Ute Indians spent the late summer and early fall in Tennessee Park, north of present-day Leadville. • Total mineral production in Lake County was $133,000 in gold and $2,036 in silver.	• Colorado's sixth railroad, the Denver, South Park and Pacific Railway Co. (DSP&P), was incorporated Oct. 1 by ex-Territorial Governor John Evans and other prominent Denver businessmen to build a narrow gauge route into the mountains and tunnel under the Continental Divide to reach the Pacific coast. • CC finally started construction in December up Clear Creek from Golden toward the mining camps of Black Hawk and Central City, Idaho Springs and Georgetown. • D&RG track reached Pueblo Aug. 1.
1873	• Malta, a small settlement at the mouth of California Gulch was started. • Hayden Survey, one of four government-sponsored scientific and mapping surveys, arrived in the area and camped at Twin Lakes. W. H. Jackson took the first known photos of Mt. Massive and Mt. of the Holy Cross. • In spite of the financial panic of 1873, Lake County mineral production reached $225,000 in gold and $3,809 in silver.	• Narrow gauge Denver, South Park & Pacific *Railway* Co. was reorganized as the Denver, South Park & Pacific *Railroad* Co. (DSP&P) to build up the South Platte River canyon, to the mining camps in southwestern Colorado and on to the Pacific coast via Yuma, Ariz. • DSP&P construction started to Morrison, Colo., in August. This branch line was built to bring coal, building stone and lumber to Denver markets. • CC continued construction from Forks Creek to Floyd Hill. The railroad also started building eastward from Golden to Longmont. • The Atchison, Topeka & Santa Fe Railroad (AT&SF), building from the east, reached Granada along the Arkan-

YEAR	LEADVILLE and COLORADO HISTORY	RAILROAD HISTORY
1873 cont.		sas River July 4. No further construction until May 1875.
		• Railroad manipulator, Jay Gould, gained control of the UP and was a member of its Board of Directors until 1885. He aimed to build up a large system of feeder railroads to support the UP system.
1874	• Malta Smelting and Mining Co. started the first smelter at Malta. • Mining engineer and metallurgist A.B. Wood and promoter W. H. Stevens formed a partnership to construct the Oro Mining Ditch and Fluming Co. to bring more water to California Gulch for large-scale placer mining. They also began acquiring claims and by 1875 controlled a large part of the gulch. • Total Lake County mineral production was $213,503 in gold and $3,575 in silver.	• In spite of the financial panic of 1873, the DSP&P completed track to Morrison by July 1, but further construction was halted until 1877. • D&RG track reached Canon City, Colo., July 4.
1875	• Wood and Stevens also began quietly searching for the source of the black carbonate ores. They filed several lode claims while continuing to wash gold from the gravels in the gulch. Assays revealed the ore contained 27% lead and 15 oz. of silver per ton. • During the winter of 1875-76, Wood and Stevens started mining the silver-rich carbonate ores at their Rock Mine (No. 78) located on a hill south of California Gulch. • The Malta smelter began handling simple ores but was never able to refine or extract (smelt) the complex metallic ores from the mined rock. • Spotswood and McClellan operated a stage line from the DSP&P railhead at Morrison to Fairplay. • Lake County mineral production in gold dropped to $43,099 while silver production increased to $20,668.	• The DSP&P spent the year trying to raise money to build to Fairplay. No construction was undertaken. • AT&SF built 84 miles from Granada to Rocky Ford. • No construction by the D&RG. HYDRAULIC MINING.

YEAR	LEADVILLE and COLORADO HISTORY	RAILROAD HISTORY
1876	• A. R. Meyer, a trained mining engineer, arrived in the district and in the fall started construction of the second smelter, the A.R. Meyer and Co. Ore Milling and Sampling Co. • S.S. Breece discovered iron ore on Breece Hill. He started the only open pit mine in the district (No. 9). • Colorado became a State Aug. 1. • Brothers John and Patrick Gallager spent the 1876-77 winter staking a number of claims and sinking a shaft. By early 1877 they hit ore that assayed 42% lead with 934 oz. of silver per ton and 4.5 oz. of gold. Among those claims were the Charleston (No. 13) and the Campbird (No. 10). During the winter of 1877-78, the Gallagers sold their properties to the St. Louis Smelting and Refining Co. for $225,000. • Tabor elected Lake County treasurer and served from 1877 to 1881. • Gold production for the year totaled $60,000, silver $26,915, and for the first time $915 in lead was reported.	• AT&SF track completed to Pueblo Feb. 29. • D&RG rails reached La Veta July 1. • The DSP&P resumed construction in October after Ex-Governor John Evans finally was able to secure much needed financing from his brother. • By the end of the year, 671 miles of standard gauge and 257 miles of narrow gauge track had been laid in Colorado.  BOTTOM OF THE SHAFT.
1877	• Leadville was born in the spring when a group of miners met to form a new town. Names suggested included Lead City, Carbonate, Meyer and Cerrusite (a lead carbonate mineral). • Town fathers petitioned for a Post Office, which opened July 16. George Henderson was first postmaster. • George A. Harris started the first hotel and Charles Mater moved his store to the new town from Granite. • Tabors, by now operating stores at both Oro City and Malta, moved both businesses to Leadville; the first Post Office was in their store. Business increased so much that Augusta no longer needed to care for boarders.	• As each new bonanza in the Leadville district was announced, Colorado's railroads began to think seriously about building to Leadville. Money was to be made hauling supplies to the town and transporting ore to Denver and eastern smelters. • During the summer, General Palmer of the D&RG and several of his officers visited Leadville and decided to build to the new mining camp at once. • In August the CC also completed track from Floyd Hill (on present-day I-70) to Georgetown. • By October, the DSP&P had completed 6 miles of grade in South Platte Canyon; plans of heading for the San Juan mining camps were sidetracked as Leadville continued to boom.

YEAR	LEADVILLE and COLORADO HISTORY	RAILROAD HISTORY
1877 cont.	• A school district was formed in July, but classes did not start until the following February. • Edwin Harrison, president of St. Louis Smelting & Refining Co., opened company offices at what would become the corner of Chestnut and Harrison Aves. Harrison started road improvements and construction of a reduction works to extract the precious metals. • Meyer's smelter was completed and fired up. • Nelson Hallock and Albert Cooper hit rich ore at 16 feet and their mine, the Carbonate (No. 11), netted the owners $250,000 the following year when they sold out. • By the fall there were at least 300 residents, a few stores and the inevitable saloons. • Three stage lines started serving Leadville via Weston Pass and the route along the Arkansas River. • Susan B. Anthony arrived in Leadville in September and gave several speeches which did little to advance the cause of women's suffrage in the State. • With new mineral strikes, Lake County gold production totaled $55,000, silver was $549,600 and lead was $66,000.	• The UP-backed CC built southward from Cheyenne via Ft. Collins and Longmont to Denver. Through service began Nov. 7.  THE SHAFT HOUSE.
1878	• Leadville city government was organized Feb. 12 and Tabor was elected mayor. At the first general election in April, he was re-elected mayor. In February Tabor was appointed postmaster, a position he had held in Kansas and also in Buckskin Joe. • On Apr. 4, George H. Fryer hit rich ore a few feet below the surface on a hill to become known as Fryer Hill. His mine, the New Discovery (No. 59), made Fryer a rich man, but he died in Denver in 1884 of an overdose of morphine.	• During the late 1870s and early 1880s, there was fierce competition among the DSP&P, D&RG, AT&SF and CC (under UP control) to be first to reach the lucrative Leadville mining district. • No one could tell from day to day which group of money manipulators controlled which railroad. Jay Gould and W.A.H. Loveland were behind a scheme to build across the Continental Divide from Georgetown, but Gould was also trying to gain control of the D&RG!

YEAR	LEADVILLE and COLORADO HISTORY	RAILROAD HISTORY
1878 cont.	• The richest deposit on Fryer Hill, the Robert E. Lee mine (No. 76), was discovered in June. • David Moffat, Marshall Field, J. B. Chaffee, and many other men made millions from Fryer Hill mines. • Tabor, who had little luck in prospecting on his own, often helped (grubstaked) down and out miners with food and supplies for a portion of any profits they might make. August Rische and George T. Hook were recipients of Tabor's generosity. The men struck paydirt on May 1 at their prospect on Fryer Hill. Their mine, the Little Pittsburg (No.44), produced $1,800,000 from 1878 to 1880. More details on Rische, Hook and Tabor are on p.115. • The Bank of Leadville organized. • Tabor elected Lt. Gov. of Colorado and served two, 2-year terms. • During 1878, newspapers, churches, banks and a volunteer fire department started. City streets were laid out and named. • David May opened his first dry goods store; best sellers were Levis and "long johns." • The first stage road between Georgetown and Leadville was completed across Loveland Pass. • Telegraph lines were strung across Mosquito Pass and reached the Leadville in December. • By the end of the year Leadville's population was estimated to be 2,000 and increasing rapidly. • Total Lake County mineral production was $60,000 in gold, $2,070,000 in silver and $360,000 in lead.	• At the same time, the AT&SF was locked in a fierce battle with the D&RG for control of Raton Pass, south of Trinidad, Colo., and of the Royal Gorge route to Leadville. The AT&SF had managed to take possession of Raton Pass late in the night of Feb. 26 by having placed a small construction crew on the pass. It was not until about 4:30 a.m. the next day that a similar crew from the D&RG arrived on the scene to find themselves outwitted. • The first AT&SF train arrived in Trinidad Sept. 1. • In a strange turn of events, on Oct. 19, D&RG bondholders leased the railroad to the AT&SF for 30 years. Gen. William J. Palmer, president of the D&RG, opposed this move and continually fought the terms of the lease. Court costs mounted as lawsuits were filed. • The AT&SF also offered to buy DSP&P stock. A clause in the lease by which the AT&SF controlled the D&RG stated that any traffic arrangements made with competing railroads would have to be approved by the D&RG. Thus the D&RG was able to stop the purchase of the stock. • Gen. Palmer again went to court and accused the AT&SF of giving secret financial aid to the DSP&P. • Jay Gould then offered to buy half the capital stock of the DSP&P but was turned down. • DSP&P laid 51 miles of track and reached Webster at the foot of Kenosha Pass by December. • Thirty miles of D&RG track was completed from Garland City to Alamosa July 4. • The CC extended its Clear Creek branch from Black Hawk to Central City.

YEAR	LEADVILLE and COLORADO HISTORY	RAILROAD HISTORY
1879	• In February Lake County seat moved from Granite to Leadville. • During the spring, more prospectors, miners, promoters, businessmen, entrepreneurs, card sharks, prostitutes, saloon keepers, wagon trains and even traveling shows arrived. • Settlers lived in tents, hastily built log cabins or board shanties. • Grubstaked miners left town either wealthy or still broke. • Cost of living was high and price for city lots skyrocketed. • Because all available timber was cut from the slopes east of town, spring runoff flooded Leadville streets regularly. • The city began installing gas lights, a water system (the pipes froze the first winter) and telephones. • The Tabor Hose Co. No. 1 was organized in February. A stock exchange began business in May. • Construction started on the Annunciation Catholic Church and the Sisters of Charity started the first St. Vincent's hospital. • During late May, a forest fire started on the north side of town; fortunately the wind changed and the town was saved. • As profits from the Little Pittsburg rolled in, Tabor bought the Chrysolite Mine (No. 15) for $10,000. Located on Fryer Hill west of the Little Pittsburg, this mine had been carefully "salted" by William H. "Chicken Bill" Lovell. Undaunted, Tabor deepened the mine and found rich ore that returned fabulous profits to Tabor and other members of a newly organized company. • By September, Tabor decided he wanted a mine to call his own and purchased the Matchless (No. 47) for	• On April 21, the U.S. Supreme Court ruled that the D&RG had prior right through the Royal Gorge, but did not deny AT&SF any right-of-way. The Arkansas River route to Leadville was still not settled. • Financial woes forced the D&RG into receivership and Jay Gould sought to purchase a half-interest in the railroad (He never did gain control of the D&RG.) At the same time, Gould was also buying DSP&P stock so he could gain control of <u>any</u> railroad built to Leadville. • A Joint Operating Agreement, negotiated by Gould, was signed Oct. 1 between the D&RG and DSP&P. Its objective was to secure peaceful coexistence between the two roads. • The D&RG was granted the right to build track from Buena Vista to Leadville and the DSP&P was granted the right to rent the D&RG trackage. The DSP&P was granted the right to build a line across Alpine Pass to Gunnison and the D&RG could rent that track. • DSP&P continued construction toward Leadville and in May completed a difficult stretch of track between Webster and the top of Kenosha Pass. Track reached Como in June and Trout Creek Pass by the end of the year. • DSP&P locating engineers completed the survey to Gunnison and contracts were awarded for construction of the Alpine Tunnel under the Continental Divide. • The CC installed a third rail between Denver and Golden, the first dual gauge in the State. • AT&SF continued to build westward from Canon City through the Royal Gorge to Texas Creek. • No D&RG construction during the year due to costly court battles.

YEAR	LEADVILLE and COLORADO HISTORY	RAILROAD HISTORY
1879 cont.	$117,000. By January 1881, this mine was producing $2,000 a day for Tabor. • In spite of his wealth, Tabor remained friends with the less fortunate and was always generous to friends, churches and charities. • Tabor Opera House opened Nov. 20 and was lighted with gas lamps from Tabor's gas company. • By years-end, 15 smelters were in operation. • Lake County mineral production was $90,000 in gold, $9,420,468 in silver and $1,774,808 in lead. • Leadville's population estimated at 7,000.	
1880	• In February rumors spread that the Little Pittsburg Mine was no longer finding rich ore. It was claimed that Chaffee and Moffat were able to unload 51,000 shares of stock before the bottom fell out of the company. Stock fell from $7.50 in mid-March to $1.95 a share in December. This crisis was brought on by overcapitalization, the need to make monthly dividend payments to stockholders, and exploitable mining practices, common to many mining companies of the day. • Lt. Gov. Horace Tabor was keeping steady company with Elizabeth McCourt Doe (Baby Doe) who first visited Leadville in 1879 and returned in the spring of 1880—without her husband, Harvey. In July, Tabor moved out of his Leadville home and tried to get a divorce from his wife, Augusta. With this transition, Tabor spent more time in Denver managing his investments and mining ventures. • An organ was hauled by mule teams across Mosquito Pass and installed in St. George's Episcopal Church. This is one of three tracker-action organs still in use in Colorado. Tracker-	• By Mar. 3, DSP&P had trains running from Trout Creek Pass to Buena Vista, crossing Trout Creek 27 times. Track was also built southward to Nathrop and westward up Chalk Creek to St. Elmo. Work continued on drilling the Alpine Tunnel. • On Mar. 27, the famous "Tripartite Agreement" was signed by the UP (which now controlled the DSP&P), the AT&SF and the D&RG. The first stipulation was cancellation of the AT&SF's lease of the D&RG and return of all stock. Receivership of the D&RG was terminated. • A second stipulation was that the AT&SF and UP agreed to not build into the mountains of central Colorado for 10 years and the D&RG was granted the right to build to Leadville on grade already finished by the AT&SF. • The final stipulation was that the D&RG was not to build south of Trinidad or Espanola, NM. The AT&SF retained the Raton Pass route. • Because Gould continued to purchase DSP&P stock, he broke the Joint Operating Agreement of 1879. Thus the

St. Vincent's Hospital. This 2-story frame building was used until 1901 when the new brick hospital was completed.   (Colorado Mountain History Collection.)

View south from the summit of Fremont Pass, showing the D&RG Blue River Extension and the small mining community of Alicante. This interesting pen and ink drawing was in Ernest Ingersoll's "Crest of the Continent," published in 1885, prior to the building the the DSP&P.

YEAR	LEADVILLE and COLORADO HISTORY	RAILROAD HISTORY
1880 cont.	action organs are quite rare because they operate entirely on mechanical rather than electric impulses. • Meyer Guggenheim came to Leadville and bought an interest in the AY (No. 1,2) and Minnie (No. 55) mines. By 1882, these mines were producing $2,000 per day. Guggenheim invested in the smelter at Pueblo, which returned additional profits. • The first miners' strike started May 26 and lasted 3 weeks when the overworked, underpaid men went back to work without gaining any concessions from mine owners. Miners worried about the the railroad reaching Leadville because it would bring many more miners, increase competition for jobs, and lower wages. • With the arrival of the railroad, many more lawyers, doctors and dentists moved to Leadville. Prices of consumer goods dropped and luxury items began to appear in the stores. The overexpanded freighting industry was badly hurt by the rail competition. • By July the district was producing 750 tons of ore per week and Leadville was the largest city in the State. • There were 14 assay offices, 10 more than the previous year. Smelters and reductions works also multiplied. • Total mineral production for Lake County was $104,014 in gold, $11,473,946 in silver and $3,332,900 in lead.	D&RG felt free to start construction of a line across Marshall Pass to Gunnison. • After the Tripartite Agreement was signed, the D&RG resumed construction along the Arkansas River from Texas Creek to Buena Vista and on to Leadville. • On July 20, the first D&RG train pulled into Leadville, thus ending 2 years of struggle and fierce competition between the railroads. • Soon after, the Blue River Extension was started, and track reached the summit of Fremont Pass Nov. 15 and Kokomo Dec. 27. • Upon completion of D&RG track to Leadville, the DSP&P started running trains from Denver to Leadville, using D&RG track between Buena Vista and Leadville. • With the arrival of the railroad, mining increased and mining costs decreased. • Even though profits soared, the DSP&P management resolved to build their own extension to Leadville via Boreas Pass. Work started on the High Line Extension in 1881 which would be 21 miles shorter than the Trout Creek-Arkansas River route. The last 14 miles eventually became the present-day Leadville, Colorado & Southern Railroad (LC&S). • The year 1880 was one of incredible expansion for the D&RG. A total of 347 miles of track was completed, including the Blue River Extension and the Eagle River Extension from Malta to Crane's Park, 10 miles north of Leadville. Also completed were the San Juan Extension from Alamosa to Chama, NM, and the New Mexico Extension between Antonito and Espanola, NM, as well as several other short branches.

YEAR	LEADVILLE and COLORADO HISTORY	RAILROAD HISTORY
1880 cont.		• The KP and DP were taken over by the UP, giving the UP control of the routes from Cheyenne to Denver.
1881	• Leadville started regular mail delivery service. • An electric generator was installed at the Billings and Eilers smelter. • The City Railway Co. started operating horse-drawn cars on Aug. 5 along Harrison Ave. from Chestnut St. to the corner of 8th and Harrison, up 8th St. to Poplar and then north to the D&RG depot. The railway was unable to operate in snow, however, because the horses could not pull the cars when ice froze in the rails. Service was suspended in July 1882. • Tabor speculated heavily in mines throughout the west, in newspapers, and banks; he even helped organize several railroads—which were never built. • Tabor Grand Opera House in Denver opened Sept. 5. • David May was elected Lake County treasurer and served two terms—his only venture into public office. • Mineral production in Lake County totaled $300,000 in gold, $9,002,039 in silver and $2,806,272 in lead. • The Colorado State Business Directory reported Leadville's population at 25,000. 	• The UP gained complete control of the DSP&P Jan. 25 when Gould sold his recently purchased stock to the UP for a tidy profit of $629,120. The UP raised freight rates immediately and traffic gradually was diverted to the D&RG. • Turbulent times for Colorado's railroads continued. In September the UP filed suit against the D&RG to prevent the latter from building along the Blue River. The D&RG claimed prior right to that route. • The DSP&P believed that since the D&RG broke the Joint Operating Agreement by starting construction across Marshall Pass, the DSP&P could build its own track to Leadville. This was the end of all agreements previously signed by the two railroads. • DSP&P started work on the branch from Como to Breckenridge and reached the top of Boreas Pass Oct. 15. • Track was completed from St. Elmo to the east portal of the Alpine Tunnel by Aug. 11. Work on digging the tunnel continued throughout the year. • The D&RG completed the 2-mile narrow gauge Fryer Hill branch to reach several mills and mines east of Leadville. • The D&RG completed the San Juan Extension from Chama, NM, to Durango, Colo., July 27. The Eagle River Extension continued from Crane's Park northward to Redcliff; the Blue River Extension was finished to Wheeler Sept. 18. The Gunnison Extension reached Gunnison in August, thus beating the DSP&P by 13 months. Other spurs and extensions added a total of 383 miles of narrow gauge track in Colorado, in addition to

Robinson, Colorado in February 1929.   *(Colorado Railroad Museum)*

Kokomo, Colorado, also in 1929. Photos were taken on the Denver Water Board Special train. Both mining camps are now covered with tailings ponds from Amax Molybdenum Mine.   *(Colorado Railroad Museum)*

YEAR	LEADVILLE and COLORADO HISTORY	RAILROAD HISTORY
1881 cont.		123 miles of third rail laid between Denver and Pueblo. The line to Salt Lake City was started. • The CC's Julesburg Branch was completed and passenger service between Denver and Omaha commenced Nov. 6. The company (under UP control) also completed the 4.5 miles of track between Georgetown and Silver Plume. • The Georgetown, Breckenridge & Leadville Railway (GB&L), a UP company, was incorporated Feb. 23 to build from Georgetown to Leadville via a tunnel under the Continental Divide in the vicinity of Loveland Pass. (Some work on a tunnel was actually done above Silver Plume.)
1882	• By the end of January, the Matchless Mine had produced about $1,500,000 for Tabor, who now spent little time in Leadville. • On May 19, fire consumed many buildings along the south side of East Chestnut St. The new First National Bank building was saved because of its brick construction. • Fire struck again May 24 when the Grant Smelter was engulfed in flames and burned to the ground. This put 300 men out of work. • Augusta Tabor filed suit in mid-April for separate maintenance, charging that Tabor had given her no financial support since the first of the year. Tabor and Baby Doe were secretly married in St. Louis, Mo., Sept. 30 after Tabor obtained a fraudulent divorce in Durango, Colo. • Mineral production in Lake County was $320,000 in gold, $10,139,765 in silver and $4,796,610 in lead. • From 1882 through 1885 the Leadville population stabilized at about 20,000 residents.	• The standard gauge Burlington & Colorado Railroad (B&C), which had reached Wray, Colo., in 1881, arrived in Denver May 29. This route eventually became the Chicago, Burlington & Quincy Railroad (CB&Q), a future owner of the DSP&P. • Breckenridge Branch of DSP&P completed 30 miles of track from the top of Boreas Pass to Breckenridge by September and to Dillon by December. • The Alpine Tunnel was completed and track reached Gunnison in September. • A DSP&P branch was also completed to Fairplay and Alma in September. The company operated 201 miles of track from Denver to Gunnison. • By 1882, the D&RG handled 85 to 90 percent of the traffic on the Buena Vista-Leadville track and the DSP&P refused to pay its share for using that track. In December the D&RG filed suit against the DSP&P to collect those fees. At the annual UP board meeting, Gov. Evans was removed as president of his beloved DSP&P railroad. After

YEAR	LEADVILLE and COLORADO HISTORY	RAILROAD HISTORY
1882 cont.		that, Evans started the Denver & New Orleans Railroad. • During the year, the D&RG spiked down 217 miles of track in Colorado. Most of the company's dwindling resources were spent on completing the Denver to Salt Lake mainline. The 11-mile Blue River Extension was completed from Wheeler to Dillon and opened for business Nov. 13.
1883	• Horace and Augusta Tabor were divorced Jan. 2. By this time, Tabor had managed to get a 30-day appointment as a U.S. Senator from Colorado. He filled the vacancy left when Sen. Henry Teller resigned to accept a cabinet post in Pres. Chester Arthur's administration. He served from Feb. 3 to Mar. 4. • On Mar. 1, Tabor and his beloved Baby Doe were married in a lavish ceremony at the Willard Hotel in Washington, DC. Pres. Arthur was in attendance. • Charles Boettcher came to Leadville from Boulder and started a hardware store. By 1883 his business had grown considerably and he organized the Leadville Light and Power Co. which began to generate electricity the following year. In later years he moved to Denver and was instrumental in starting the Colorado Portland Cement Co and the Great Western Sugar Co. • Mineral production in Lake County reached an all-time high with $400,000 in gold, $10,044,633 in silver and $4,797,725 in lead.	• In May the DSP&P agreed to a settlement of the suit filed by the D&RG the year before. • On Aug. 3, the DSP&P (UP) started construction from Dillon to Leadville. Details of the High Line construction are on p. 10. • Only other DSP&P construction during the year was from Gunnison northward to the coal mines at Baldwin and some track up Ohio Creek. • The D&RG completed only 33 miles of narrow gauge track in Colorado during the year. The mainline to Salt Lake opened for business April 8. • The D&RG obtained the approval of the Lake County commissioners to build a 3-mile spur to AY #2 (No. 1) and Minnie (No. 55) mines in California Gulch and thus obtained a monopoly on transporting ore from those mines to smelters. • The Colorado Midland Railway Co. (CM) was incorporated Nov. 23 to build a standard gauge railroad from Colorado Springs, through Ute Pass to South Park and to Leadville. Construction started in 1886.
1884	• Few who came to Leadville became wealthy. Most struggled, working long hours at low wages under extremely difficult conditions.	• Problems between the D&RG and DSP&P continued. On Feb. 1, the roundhouse in Leadville, used jointly by the two railroads, was destroyed by fire and five D&RG locomotives and one DSP&P locomotive were badly damaged.

YEAR	LEADVILLE and COLORADO HISTORY	RAILROAD HISTORY
1884 cont.	• The Lake County Miners Union was organized. It became the Knights of Labor in 1889. • Total Lake County mineral production included $500,000 in gold, $8,070,047 in silver, $3,464,236 in lead; and for the first time, $13,000 in copper was produced. 	• The High Line Extension of the DSP&P was finally completed to Leadville on Feb. 5, but regular train service did not begin until Sept. 30. • This new route was 126 miles shorter than the D&RG route via Pueblo and Salida, but operations through the years proved much more difficult because the Continental Divide was crossed twice. • When the DSP&P reached Leadville, the mining boom had already peaked, so the volume of freight traffic was much less than expected. The costs of building and operating the High Line across Boreas and Fremont Passes coupled with UP mismanagement forced the DSP&P into receivership. • The D&RG, heavily in debt because of recent expansion, went into receivership July 12. No construction was completed except for a tunnel and alignment changes near Bridgeport. • The Georgetown, Breckenridge & Leadville (GB&L) extended the CC track 8 miles from Georgetown via the famous Georgetown Loop to Silver Plume and on to Graymont. • CM articles of incorporation were amended Oct. 7 to build branches to Aspen, Fairplay and Alma and to the western border of Colorado with a main range tunnel under the Continental Divide at Hagerman Pass.
1885	• The Tabor Grand Hotel in Leadville opened. • Tabor's fortune began to decline because of his free-spending and many poor investments. • In the Leadville District, the high-grade ores found close to the surface were depleted. Mines were deepened and smelters began to develop ways to	• The DSP&P completed a new connection between Nathrop and their main line across Trout Creek Pass. • Heavy snows blocked Boreas Pass for 3 months, and the DSP&P was again forced to use the D&RG track to Leadville from Buena Vista. • By 1885, 285 railroads had been incorporated within the State of Colorado.

YEAR	LEADVILLE and COLORADO HISTORY	RAILROAD HISTORY
1885 cont.	recover the more complex assemblages of ore minerals found at greater depths. • As mines were deepened, water seeping into the shafts made mining much more difficult and expensive. • Demand for minerals declined throughout the United States. • Cone-shaped stone kilns were built in the Arkansas Valley to make charcoal for use as a flux in the smelters. All available timber was cut, leading to further erosion on the hillsides surrounding Leadville. • At one time 2,500 men worked to produce needed charcoal. • Lake County mineral production dropped again with $570,000 in gold, $6,892,612 in silver, $2,165,358 in lead, $10,800 in copper and for the first time, $2,150 in zinc was produced.	• CM elected John J. Hagerman president and he set out to secure needed capital so construction could begin. 
1886	• Total mineral production in Lake County was $433,691 in gold, $6,421,187 in silver, $3,882,400 in lead, $11,100 in copper and $2,200 in zinc. • Leadville's population dropped to about 7,500 residents. 	• Contracts were awarded April 6 for the first construction of the CM from Colorado Springs. Three miles of track was laid to Colorado City and 8 tunnels on Ute Pass were completed. Work also started east from Leadville but this arrangement did not last long because both the D&RG and DSP&P charged the CM exorbitant prices to transport all equipment, supplies and even disassembled standard gauge locomotives. Work also started on the Hagerman Tunnel. • D&RG, still in receivership, was sold by its bondholders at a foreclosure sale July 12. The railroad was then reorganized as the Denver & Rio Grande *Railroad* Co. • Both the D&RG and DSP&P worried about CM construction to Leadville and the competition that a standard gauge line would bring.

YEAR	LEADVILLE and COLORADO HISTORY	RAILROAD HISTORY
1887	• In spite of an 1884 agreement between the UP, D&RG, CB&Q and AT&SF, the UP railroad reduced shipping rates for ore from Leadville mines to their Denver and Omaha smelters. As a result, less than half the furnaces in Leadville operated during 1887-88. • Mineral production in Lake County continued a slow decline with $243,694, in gold, $5,874,438 in silver, $4,156,160 in lead, $27,600 in copper and $2,300 in zinc being reported.	• During the year, the D&RG built 148 miles of branches, including the one from Glenwood Springs to Aspen—thus beating the CM to that mining town. • D&RG built a 3-mile cutoff between Leadville and Leadville Junction so ore and coal trains from Aspen could go directly to smelters in Leadville. • CM track reached Leadville Aug. 30. The Hagerman Tunnel was completed and track reached Glenwood Springs Dec. 18. The branch from Basalt to Maroon was also completed. • In the 222 miles between Colorado Springs and Newcastle, Colo., the CM built 17 tunnels and several high trestles—all standard gauge. • In Leadville, the CM built an 8-stall roundhouse, a coal tipple, sandhouse and a beautiful two-story depot.
1888	• Total mineral production in Lake County was $310,891 in gold, $5,156,900 in silver, $3,228,639 in lead, $33,600 in copper and $7,350 in zinc. • The price of silver began to drop because of increased production and a worldwide decrease in demand. Western silver miners began to demand government price supports. THE JIG DRILL.	• In order to compete with the standard gauge CM, the D&RG continued to add a standard gauge third rail to their mainline at locations throughout the State. • Several short branches to coal and metal mines added 7 miles of new track for the D&RG. • Because the DSP&P had failed to earn even the interest on its bonds since 1883, the railroad was placed in receivership in May. This was due partly to UP mis-management. • The CM completed the line to Aspen Feb. 4 and extended the main line from Glenwood Springs to Newcastle by Oct. 15. • CM surveys were started to build a new tunnel under the Continental Divide that would be 7.5 miles shorter, have gentler grades and be lower than the Hagerman Tunnel. • The Aspen Short Line Railroad (ASL)—a CM company—was incorporated

YEAR	LEADVILLE and COLORADO HISTORY	RAILROAD HISTORY
1888 cont.		Nov. 11 to build a 6.5-mile cutoff from Crystal Lake to Leadville, thus reducing grades from 3.8-percent to 1.6-percent.
1889	• The Presbyterian Church, at 8th and Harrison Sts., was completed and a Schuelke tracker-action organ was installed. The only other organ of this type in Colorado is in Boulder. • Tabor, heavily in debt, was forced to work in the Vulture Mine in Arizona in which he had unwisely invested large sums of money. • Water in mines became a more serious problem. A. A. Blow began digging a tunnel from California Gulch to his property on Iron Hill to drain the mines. The Blow Tunnel was about 4,000 feet long when purchased by the Yak Mining and Milling and Tunnel Co, headed by A. A. Meyer. This tunnel, the Yak (No. 92), was extended and in 1904 made contact with the Ibex No. 4 Mine (No. 35), 2 miles from the mouth of the drainage tunnel. • American Smelting and Refining Company (Asarco) formed. • Coke replaced charcoal in the smelting plants. • Lake County mineral production included $189,397 in gold, $5,781,789 in silver, $3,267,651 in lead, $35,976 in copper and $7,500 in zinc. • Leadville City Directory reported a population of 6,680 residents.	• In March the DL&G got its first rotary snowplow, which was immediately put to work clearing huge snowdrifts near and in Leadville. • The D&RG completed several more branches, which added 70 miles of track to the system, and 3-rail trackage was reduced by 39 miles. • The ASL completed the cutoff in mid-June and the CM leased the line for $8,000 a year until 1893 when the CM purchased the route. • In August, the DSP&P was reorganized as the Denver, Leadville & Gunnison Railway (DL&G) but continued to be completely owned by the UP. • The Rio Grande Southern Railroad (RGS) was incorporated in October.
1890	• The Federal government began to bolster the silver market with the Sherman Silver Purchase Act, enacted on July 14. The Sherman Act repealed the Bland-Allison Act and authorized the government to purchase 4.5 million ounces of silver per month and issue U.S. treasury notes.in payment. The notes were legal tender and redeemable in either gold or silver.	• In April, the DL&G sent the new rotary snowplow to Alpine Pass to try to open that line, which had been blocked for weeks. In 3 days, the plow completed the job not possible with the older Jull Centrifugal Snow Excavator. • Somehow, the DL&G managed to buy eight new narrow gauge locomotives, for use on the former South Park track.

YEAR	LEADVILLE and COLORADO HISTORY	RAILROAD HISTORY
1890 cont.	• The Sherman Act also required the United States to maintain both gold and silver on a parity with each other based upon a legal ratio of 16 to 1. • Because of the lower price of silver, many foreign governments discontinued their purchase of silver, and foreign investors selling American securities demanded gold in payment. • Some U.S. smelters that had been buying foreign metals were forced to close. • Leadville's population increased slightly to about 7,200 residents. • Lake County mineral production included $295,063 in gold, $5,579,627 in silver, $1,963,056 in lead, $275,501 in copper and $8,250 in zinc. 	These 2-8-0s, numbered 266-273, were later to become C&S engines numbered 63-70. • Also in April, 12 railroad companies controlled by the UP were combined into a single system called the Union Pacific, Denver & Gulf Railway Co. (UPD&G). Among those remotely connected with the railroads to Leadville were the CC and GB&L. The UP was almost bankrupt. • The D&RG completed new track alignment from Leadville to Pando and constructed a tunnel under Tennessee Pass. With the conversion to standard gauge between Denver and Grand Junction via Leadville, the DL&G could not compete with the D&RG's new, improved service that included Pullmans (sleeping cars), dining cars and faster schedules. • The Busk Tunnel Railway Co. (BT) was incorporated June 16 to build the Busk-Ivanhoe Tunnel which would be 581 feet lower and 7,234 feet longer than the Hagerman Tunnel. This route would avoid the steep 4-percent climb to the tunnel and huge, curving timber trestles. Tunnel portals were at Busk station on the eastern side and Ivanhoe on the western side of the Continental Divide.
1891	• The price of silver dropped from a high of $1.29 per ounce to $0.99 per ounce. • Mine shafts began to be dug within the city limits of Leadville, and good ore was found at 200 to 300 feet. • Total mineral production in Lake County dropped again with $348,419 in gold, $4,745,085 in silver, $2,298,134 in lead, $581,658 in copper and $7,500 in zinc being reported.	• Standard gauge D&RG locomotives began pulling narrow gauge trains between Leadville and Denver. Only one branch was completed during the year, because the D&RG was involved in financing a subsidiary, the fabled Rio Grande Southern Railroad (RGS).

YEAR	LEADVILLE and COLORADO HISTORY	RAILROAD HISTORY
1892	• The "downtown" district became the center of mining activity. • Price of silver dropped to $0.87 per ounce. • Grover Cleveland elected president. He was a firm believer in the gold standard and thought the country's financial problems were due to the government's purchase of silver. • Lake County mineral production included $251,296 in gold, $5,131,277 in silver, $1,760,365 in lead, $687,748 in copper and $25,875 in zinc.	
1893	• India was the most important silver market in the world, and in June the mints in that country closed because of low prices. This precipitated the Panic of 1893 that closed many banks and silver mines throughout the west and brought on a severe depression. • Of the 70 to 90 silver-producing mines in the district, only 18 remained open after the crash. Many businesses, smelters, and one bank in Leadville closed. • A special session of the U. S. Congress convened Aug. 1 and in October the Sherman Silver Purchase Act was repealed. No longer would silver be on a parity with gold any more than with nickel or copper. • By the end of August, the Colorado labor commissioner reported that of the total State population of 450,000, more than 45,000 were out of work. • In September, miners agreed to a reduction in pay from $3.00 to $2.50 per day for those months in which the price of silver was less than $0.835 per ounce. • Mines reopened by the end of the year, but much time and money had to be spent in pumping out water.	• The BT completed the Busk-Ivanhoe Tunnel Dec. 17. The new track was then leased to the CM. Many problems were encountered in drilling the tunnel and many men were killed. • The UP, AT&SF and CM were forced into bankruptcy by the financial panic. Somehow, the D&RG managed to survive. • DL&G earnings for the year dropped by one-third. Nevertheless, a new brick depot was completed in Leadville. This building is now the depot for the Leadville, Colorado & Southern Railroad (LC&S). 

YEAR	LEADVILLE and COLORADO HISTORY	RAILROAD HISTORY
1893 cont.	• Many who had made millions in mining were left penniless, including Tabor. He went to Mexico and worked in a mine in the Jesus Maria District—another investment venture that never produced the expected riches. Tabor and Baby Doe lived in poverty until he was appointed Denver postmaster, a year before his death in 1899. On his deathbed he made Baby Doe promise to "hang onto the Matchless Mine," thinking it would again produce rich ore. She died at the mine in 1935. • August Rische also lost most of his fortune and spent the balance of his life prospecting, mining and hoping to find another Little Pittsburg. • Lake County mineral production included $902,244 in gold, $5,300,455 in silver, $1,342,171 in lead, $540,000 in copper and $29,400 in zinc.	 FIRST STAGE.—ADJUSTING THE PACK.
1894	• The price of silver bottomed out at $0.61 per ounce. Without the mines that still produced gold, copper, lead and manganese, Leadville would have become a ghost town. • The Little Jonny Mine (No. 43), located on the upper slopes of Stray Horse Gulch, was developed by John F. Campion and named for his infant son, Johnny. Somehow, the name was recorded without the "h." • By the 1890s, the mine was owned by the Ibex Mining Company; Campion was general manager and J. J. Brown was superintendent. Brown had worked his way up from miner to shift boss, timberman and foreman. He studied geology and ore deposition and developed a technique to sink a shaft through sand and dolomite to tap the rich gold and copper deposits below. This mine produced some $13 million in gold between 1893 and 1923. Brown is also remembered as the husband of Maggie Tobin Brown, the	• The CM went into receivership Feb. 2. • More hard times for Colorado's railroads. The D&RG suffered further financial setbacks due to a disastrous flood in the Arkansas River valley. • Train timetable showed 16 passenger trains served Leadville.

YEAR	LEADVILLE and COLORADO HISTORY	RAILROAD HISTORY
1894 cont.	"unsinkable" Molly Brown who survived the 1912 sinking of the passenger ship, Titanic, on its maiden voyage from Europe to the U.S. • Lake County mineral production was $1,499,314 in gold, $4,847,918 in silver, $1,476,189 in lead, $380,000 in copper and $35,000 in zinc.	
1895	• The gray metallic mineral found on Bartlett Mountain was finally identified as molybdenite by Prof. George of the Colorado School of Mines. • This was a profitable year for Leadville. Silver production was the highest since the boom year of 1880 and gold production also increased. • Total Lake County mineral production rebounded somewhat with $1,386,359 in gold, $6,133,018 in silver, $1,245,522 in lead, $299,980 in copper and $45,540 in zinc. • Population in Leadville increased to about 7,700. • The Panic of 1893 was over and there was little unemployment, although some miners were still paid only $2.50 for 10-hour days. • In May the Western Federation of Miners established the Cloud City Local No. 33 to organize miners to demand a pay increase; the other union, Knights of Labor, had lost much influence with its members. The new union wanted miners to receive more of the bounty from the largest mining district in Colorado. • To celebrate the new prosperity and publicize Leadville, it was decided to host a winter carnival and build a monumental ice palace that would cover more than 3 acres. It was located west of Maple St. between 7th and 8th Sts. The cornerstone for this huge	• The DL&G managed to build a spur track from Kokomo to Wilfley's Mill. • The D&RG could afford little maintenance for the entire system. • Receiver for the AT&SF was discharged.  TOSSING THE FLAPJACK.

86

YEAR	LEADVILLE and COLORADO HISTORY	RAILROAD HISTORY
1895 cont.	Norman-style castle was laid Nov. 25. A spell of unseasonably warm weather in December almost killed the project.	
1896	• Large blocks of ice were cut from nearby lakes and hauled to the building site on sleds pulled by teams of horses. Additional ice was brought to Leadville from Palmer Lake, near Colorado Springs, by the D&RG. As construction continued, water was sprayed on the blocks which then froze and held the walls together. • The 350x450-foot building had 90-foot towers which graced the main entrance with many parapets and smaller towers. Inside the ice was a frame building with a roof of ice crystals and steel. There were a large ice rink, heated dining rooms and a ballroom. • The Ice Palace opened Jan. 1 with a grand parade through Leadville. The palace lasted until Mar. 28 when the ice began to melt. Thousands visited the Cloud City to see the largest such structure ever built. There were skating exhibitions, ice sculptures, rock drilling contests and many more activities for visitors. Financially, the ice palace was a failure but it brought Leadville much publicity. • By mid-June the Western Federation of Miners Local No. 33 had 2,600 members. The union demanded shorter working hours and a uniform $3 per day wage. Mine owners refused and June 19, miners voted to strike. • Mines were closed to all but pump men, firemen and engineers. In August several mines decided to reopen and pay the old wages. The Coronado Mine (No. 18) reopened Aug. 17 and on Sept. 20, the mine was wracked by gunfire and an explosion. The resulting fire killed three men and destroyed	

Main entrance to the Ice Palace, guarded by "Lady Leadville," who was pointing to the mountains from whence Leadville's wealth had come. (W. H. Jackson, Colorado Mountain History Collection)

Interior of game exhibit room. Stuffed mammals of Colorado were displayed, along with an exhibit by the D&RG Railroad.

(W. H. Jackson, Colorado Mountain History Collection)

Huge piles of snow were still standing along Harrison Avenue in the spring following the bad winter of 1898-1899. *(Colorado Historical Society)*

YEAR	LEADVILLE and COLORADO HISTORY	RAILROAD HISTORY
1896 cont.	most of the mine buildings and shaft house. • After that fracas, the Colorado Militia arrived in Leadville to restore order. The arrival of scab miners from Missouri, did little to cool hot tempers. • The strike lasted until Mar. 9, 1897, when weary, dejected miners voted to go back to work without gaining any concessions from the long, bitter strike. • The strike forced one Leadville bank to close along with many other businesses. It took 2 years to drain the mines that were not pumped during the 8-month strike. • Tabor Grand Opera House and adjoining office building in Denver were sold at a sheriff's sale June 23. • Total Lake County mineral production was $1,453,458 in gold, $4,504,160 in silver, $959,813 in lead, $439,750 in copper and $25,038 in zinc.	
1897	• Mineral production in Lake County included $2,063,858 in gold, $3,270,790 in silver, $853,233 in lead, $377,616 in copper and $90,262 in zinc.	• The CM was sold at foreclosure sale Sept. 8 and then reorganized. Because leasing the Busk-Ivanhoe Tunnel from the builders was so costly, the CM started using the Hagerman Pass Tunnel again in November. Attempts were also made to become more competitive with the D&RG. • The DL&G built a covered turntable and engine house at Climax; three new engines (Nos. 9-11, which in later years became UPD&G Nos. 71-73) were delivered, the last new locomotives ever used on the line. • Four DL&G passenger trains operated between Denver and Leadville. Train No.1, a daily mail and express, left Denver at 8:15 a.m., arrived at Climax at 4:45 p.m., and Leadville at 5:30 p.m.. Train No. 2 left Leadville at 9 a.m., and arrived in Denver at 6:05 p.m.. The mixed daily (except Sunday),

YEAR	LEADVILLE and COLORADO HISTORY	RAILROAD HISTORY
1897 cont.		Train No 11, left Denver at 6:30 p.m. and arrived in Leadville at 7:00 a.m. the following morning. Train No. 12 left Leadville at 1:00 p.m., arrived at Climax at 2:15 p.m., and in Denver the following morning at 4:00 a.m.
1898	• Spanish-American War began Apr. 25. • The winter of 1898-99 was one of the worst on record in Colorado and many mountain towns were completely isolated. In Leadville, many mines were forced to close and 2,000 men were laid off when needed coal, food and supplies could not be delivered because trains were buried in snowdrifts. • Mineral production in Lake County included $2,073,036 in gold, $4,170,550 in silver, $1,365,910 in lead, $687,450 in copper and $122,981 in zinc. **"THE COLORADO ROAD"** CS& The Colorado & Southern Ry. Co.	• The Leadville Mineral Belt Railway Co. (LMB) was incorporated Oct. 28 to build 2.9 miles southward from a junction with the main lines of the DL&G, (MP 149.90, to mines in Fryer Hill and Graham Park areas. Under control by the DL&G, construction started on the dual gauge route that had many side branches and spurs to famous mines in the area. The line connected with both the D&RG and CM at the southern edge of Leadville. • The D&RG built the 7-mile Chrysolite Extension from Leadville east up Big Evans Gulch to such famous mines as the Little Jonny (No. 43, later owned by Ibex), Resurrection (No. 72,73), New Monarch (No. 60) and Penn (No. 64-66). Track was completed Nov. 24 and reached 11,522 feet, the highest elevation reached by the D&RG. • With the UP in bankruptcy, the DL&G was sold at foreclosure on Nov. 18. On Dec. 19, the Colorado & Southern Railway Co. (C&S) was organized by holders of UPD&G and DL&G securities. The Chicago, Burlington & Quincy Railroad (CB&Q) was also involved in the financial manipulations of this sale.
1899	• Between Jan. 1 and Mar. 28, 187 inches of snow fell in Leadville and much more on the mountains around town. But through it all, the Leadville schools managed to stay open. • Two miners, trapped for 2 weeks in the Bon Air Mine (No. 8), were rescued Mar. 23. Meltwater from the heavy snows caused a cave-in at the mine.	• The C&S assumed control of the DL&G and the UPD&G Jan. 12. Included in this transfer was 328 miles of track between Denver, Leadville and Gunnison and 55 miles of track from Denver to Silver Plume. (Track to Graymont had been abandoned in 1898.)

YEAR	LEADVILLE and COLORADO HISTORY	RAILROAD HISTORY
1899 cont.	• During the year several smelting companies combined to form the American Smelting and Refining Co. The Guggenheims were asked to join, but declined; they managed to make more money that year with their 3 plants than AS&R made with 20 plants. Needless to say, the Guggenheims were again invited to join at much more favorable terms. • In Leadville, the Meyer smelter and the Bi-Metallic smelter joined the AS&R group. • Zinc ore from the Moyer Mine (No. 58) was shipped to Belgium for processing. By 1901 two zinc processing plants had been built in Colorado which greatly reduced the cost of refining zinc. • Horace Tabor died Apr. 10 at the Windsor Hotel in Denver of peritonitis. He was 69. • Lake County mineral production included $2,196,498 in gold, $4,388,071 in silver, $2,186,942 in lead, $547,684 in copper and $613,364 in zinc.	• The C&S between Como and Leadville was blocked by snowslides and snowdrifts from 30 to 40 feet deep that kept the line closed for 122 days. The route was finally reopened May 25. • The C&S still operated four passenger trains between Denver and Leadville. Train No. 71, the daily mail and express, left Denver at 8:15 a.m. and arrived in Leadville at 6:40 p.m., an hour and ten minutes later than the 1897 schedule. Train No. 72, left Leadville at 7:30 a.m. and arrived in Denver only 5 minutes later than the 1897 schedule. Train No. 81, the mixed daily (except Sunday) followed the same schedule as the 1897 DL&G timetable. Train No. 82 from Leadville to Denver, left Leadville at 7:45 a.m. and arrived in Denver at 11:20 p.m. instead of 4:00 a.m. • In February, miners were paid $1.75 per day to shovel snow off the D&RG track between Malta and Leadville. A D&RG train on the Blue River Branch was caught in an avalanche. • CM kept the route through the Hagerman Tunnel operating until Jan. 27 when the line was blocked for 77 days by huge snowdrifts. Four engines were buried in the snow and passenger service did not resume until April 16. • On June 21, the CM purchased the Busk-Ivanhoe Tunnel, and the higher route was abandoned. This was the first of many abandonments to come in the 1900s.
1900	• Completion of rail spurs to the mines, begun in 1898, reduced freight rates. • A better year for mineral production in Lake County. A total of $2,529,512 in gold, $4,319,713 in silver, $2,754,385 in lead, $452,940 in copper and $635,404 in zinc were reported.	• Construction was completed on the narrow gauge 2.9 mile LMB track to the Robert E. Lee (No.76), the Robert Emmett (No. 75), Blind Tom (No. 6) and Moduc (No. 56) and other mines in Graham Park. This track was later changed to dual gauge.

YEAR	LEADVILLE and COLORADO HISTORY	RAILROAD HISTORY
1900 cont.	• The State Business Directory reported total Leadville population as 15,000, while the Leadville City Directory listed only 9,181 residents.	• Dual gauge track was built south from the C&S station to the Bon Air (No. 8) and other mines and also connected with CM and D&RG track. After completion, the company was sold to the C&S for $15,377.23. • The D&RG built 2 miles of narrow gauge track from Graham Park Junction to the Wolftone (No. 90) and other mines. • The D&RG, Rio Grande Western (RGW) and C&S purchased the CM in July and the following year the D&RG bought out the portion owned by the RGW, giving the two railroads access to the booming Cripple Creek gold fields.
1901	• Gas lights on city streets were converted to electricity. • Five smelters were in operation. • The second St. Vincent's hospital opened. • Lake County mineral production totaled $1,776,132 in gold, $4,098,050 in silver, $2,423,467 in lead, $322,403 in copper and $949,853 in zinc.	
1902	• The Tabor Opera House in Leadville, which had become the Weston Opera House, was remodeled and opened Dec. 11 as the Elks Opera House. • Mineral production in Lake County totaled $1,203,924 in gold, $2,990,184 in silver, $1,617,457 in lead, $318,562 in copper and zinc production jumped to $2,286,600.	• The C&S used practically the same schedule for passenger trains running between Denver and Leadville as the DL&G had used in 1897. • Edwin T. Hawley and a group of investors acquired the C&S during the year.
1903	• Lake County mineral production totaled $1,339,974 in gold, $2,685,438 in silver, $1,526,836 in lead, $350,252 in copper and a whopping $4,134,064 in zinc.	• The dining room in the CM depot was closed. The building was removed in the late 1930s. • During the early 1900s, the C&S ran a daylight passenger train from Denver to Leadville with a return at night as a mixed (passenger-freight) train.

YEAR	LEADVILLE and COLORADO HISTORY	RAILROAD HISTORY
1904	• The Yak drainage tunnel, now 2 miles long, reached the Ibex No. 4 Mine. • The Yak powerplant was completed in October. • Lake County mineral production totaled $1,186,851 in gold, $2,949,388 in silver, $2,028,777 in lead, $478,028 in copper and $2,970,972 in zinc.	
1906	• The Yak powerplant produced enough electric power to supply the city with electricity. • Lake County mineral production totaled $1,508,410 in gold, $2,645,430 in silver, $2,705,047 in lead, $403,898 in copper and $4,282,106 in zinc.	• The CM abandoned 5 miles of the original main line from Snowden to Leadville and the Leadville traffic was routed via Arkansas Junction.
1907	• Panic of 1907, although not as severe as earlier financial depressions, dried up the market for metals and the downtown mines were again allowed to flood. • Lake County mineral production totaled $1,064,690 in gold, $2,742,243 in silver, $1,723,549 in lead, $535,902 in copper and $3,967,595 in zinc.	• Electric transmission lines were completed to Leadville, greatly reducing the need for coal shipments to Leadville.
1908	• Lake County mineral production totaled $1,228,449 in gold, $$1,533,553 in silver, $825,132 in lead, $617,034 in copper and $1,089,840 in zinc. • Total Leadville population listed as 13,000 in the State Business Directory.	• CM's financial woes continued, but the railroad managed to survive until 1921 when it was forced into abandonment. • On July 31, the D&RG merged with the RGW to form the consolidated Denver & Rio Grande Railroad Co. (D&RG). • A washout in Trout Creek Canyon Aug. 1 destroyed about 1 mile of C&S track which was partly relocated and rebuilt by October. • On Dec 21, the CB&Q purchased the C&S from the Hawley interests. With this transaction, the CB&Q controlled 2,000 miles of track and through its alliance with the Great Northern (GN) and Northern Pacific (NP) now had a

YEAR	LEADVILLE and COLORADO HISTORY	RAILROAD HISTORY
1908 cont.		direct route from the Pacific Northwest to Galveston, Tex. • CB&Q operated the C&S as a subsidiary until 1970 when it merged with the Burlington Northern Railroad (BN).
1910	• The Wolftone Mine (No. 90), first opened in the 1880s, held a fancy banquet for 250 invited guests in the underground workings of the mine to celebrate the renewed mining activity of its zinc-rich ores. • Rische died in Denver of pneumonia at the age of 76. • Fish hatchery started. • Lake County mineral production totaled $1,213,134 in gold, $1,793,888 in silver, $846,987 in lead, $462,935 in copper and $3,043,842 in zinc.	• A cave-in at the Alpine Tunnel in October closed the route to Gunnison and all C&S track west of the Arkansas River Valley. • More washouts between Trout Creek Pass and Buena Vista closed that line forever, and on Oct. 31, service across Boreas Pass was suspended. Four disconnected sections were left—from Breckenridge to Leadville, from Buena Vista to Hancock, from Quartz to Baldwin, and from Denver to Como. This was the end of Como as a division point. • Another cave-in at Tennessee Pass tunnel forced D&RG trains to use CM track between Snowden and Newcastle for a short time. • C&S employees timetable effective Oct. 5, lists only second class mixed trains operating between Leadville and Denver and return. Train No. 80 left Denver at 7:50 a.m. daily and arrived in Leadville at 8:30 p.m. Train No. 81 left Leadville at 7:30 a.m. and arrived in Denver at 7:55 p.m.
1911	• Lake County mineral production totaled $1,133,442 in gold, $1,593,867 in silver, $832,459 in lead, $502,188 in copper and $4,081,796 in zinc. • Leadville's population dropped to 10,000 residents, according to the State Business Directory.	• Mining continued to decline all over Colorado and narrow gauge branches began to be abandoned. • In a rare cooperative agreement, the C&S leased the Baldwin branch to the D&RG and the C&S took over operation of all traffic on the Blue River Branch between Leadville and Dillon. However, no trains were ever run on the D&RG track after February by either railroad. The C&S continued to operate daily passenger service from Leadville to Breckenridge.

View south along Harrison Avenue from 8th Street in about 1910. The Delaware Hotel is the 3-story building on the corner with the awning. Note the large tin coffee pot on the roof of the local hardware store.

(George L. Beam photo, Courtesy Jackson C. Thode)

George L. Beam, D&RG photographer, took this view of Leadville from the east end of 7th St. in about 1915. Mt. Massive is on the skyline. Due east of the church spire is the roof of the C&S railroad depot. (George L. Beam photo, Courtesy Jackson C. Thode)

Another interesting panorama of long-ago Leadville looks west from 3rd Street.
(George L. Beam photo, Courtesy Jackson C. Thode)

View east of the Little Jonny and surrounding mines. The railroad track belongs to the D&RG which reached the mine through a series of loops and switchbacks.
(Colorado Historical Society)

YEAR	LEADVILLE and COLORADO HISTORY	RAILROAD HISTORY
1911 cont.		• D&RG took over operation of C&S track between Quartz, Gunnison and Baldwin. D&RG also built a short spur to connect the two tracks betwen Parlin and Quartz.
1912		• The C&S sold its portion of the CM to a New York company, but the D&RG kept its 50% ownership. The CM remained in receivership.
1913	• Lake County mineral production totaled $1,023,631 in gold, $2,053,792 in silver, $1,288,592 in lead, $298,218 in copper and $5,255,200 in zinc.	• The D&RG added a third rail to the Graham Park and Wolftone branches. • The C&S resumed service across Boreas Pass to Leadville which continued until the final abandonment in 1937.
1915	• Mines that had been shut down since the Panic of 1907 were finally drained and brought back into production. • Fryer Hill mines were drained by a project in the Harvard Shaft. • Leadville's first smelter for zinc ores, Western Zinc Oxide Co., opened and shipped refined ores. • Chemists and metallurgists finally found a way to separate molybdenum from the complex ores at the Climax Mine. The first shipment of 6,000 pounds of molybdenum sulfide brought an incredible $2,525 per ton. • Colorado passed the prohibition amendment to the State Constitution; Lake County residents voted against the amendment by a 2 to 1 margin. • Lake County mineral production totaled $2,246,152 in gold, $1,303,498 in silver, $984,998 in lead, $315,599 in copper and $8,989,154 in zinc.	• The C&S petitioned to abandon the route between Denver and Leadville, but turned down by the Interstate Commerce Commission (ICC). The company did remove the water tanks at Gunnison and Parlin because they were no longer used.
1916	• When the Prohibition Amendment went into effect Jan. 1, 50 saloons closed in Leadville and by late summer they were replaced with "soft drink	

YEAR	LEADVILLE and COLORADO HISTORY	RAILROAD HISTORY
1916 cont.	parlors." But liquor was still available "for medicinal purposes." • The Columbine Brewery in Leadville closed, throwing many men out of work. • American Metal Co. took options on a number of molybdenum claims on Bartlett Mountain. • Lake County mineral production reached an all-time high of $1,720,440 in gold, $1,928,783 in silver, $1,498,638 in lead, $644,932 in copper and zinc production totaled $10,289,256.	
1917	• The U.S. entered World War I by declaring war on Germany, Apr. 6. • Lake County mineral production totaled $1,175,219 in gold, $1,799,616 in silver, $1,573,955 in lead, $595,856 in copper and $6,145,942 in zinc. • Leadville population was down to 7,508 according to the State Business Directory.	• D&RG track from Leadville to Graham Park Junction and to Ibex was converted to standard gauge. • CM was sold at foreclosure sale in April to A. E. Carlton and Spencer Penrose of Colorado Springs. The Colorado Midland *Railroad* Co. was incorporated May 31 as a successor to the Colorado Midland *Railway* Co. • The U.S. Railroad Administration (USRA) took over control and operation of all U.S. railroads for the duration of World War I.
1918	• The Yak Tunnel, now 3 1/2 miles long, reached the Resurrection No. 2 Mine (No. 73). This massive project drained many mines along the way. • Mines, even marginally profitable ones, were worked successfully from this tunnel and paid the Yak Mining, Milling and Tunnel Co. for the opportunity. • The Yak Tunnel provided its owners a steady income for 50 years. • Three separate companies were working claims on Bartlett Mountain but finally sold out to Climax Molybdenum Co. after heated court fights. • By the end of the World War I, the mine on Bartlett Mountain was pro-	• The D&RG again went into receivership Jan. 26. • In May, the USRA announced that due to "operational difficulties," all through traffic previously assigned to CM would be transferred to the D&RG. This was the final blow for the CM. • On Aug. 14, the last CM passenger train left Grand Junction and arrived in Colorado Springs the next day. The spur track to mines in the Leadville District was also abandoned.

YEAR	LEADVILLE and COLORADO HISTORY	RAILROAD HISTORY
1918 cont.	ducing the world's supply of molybdenum, but after the war the market dropped sharply and the mine shut down in 1919. • Flu epidemic arrived in Leadville in October and by the end of the year 223 people had died. Worldwide, 30 million people died. • Lake County mineral production totaled $843,239 in gold, $2,290,121 in silver, $1,595,364 in lead, $401,754 in copper and $4,251,132 in zinc.	
1919	• Inflation was up after the war but miners' wages were cut $1 per day. This precipitated a strike, but the men went back to work 3 days later after accepting the cut in pay. • After the end of World War I, metal prices dropped and mining never recovered. • Lake County mineral production totaled $625,956 in gold, $1,727,403 in silver, $598,851 in lead, $165,285 in copper and $1,691,061 in zinc.	• The CM abandoned the Aspen Branch and the short branch between Leadville and Arkansas Junction. • The D&RG continued to be operated by the USRA and its finances were administered by the U.S. courts.
1920	• Lake County mineral production totaled $768,365 in gold, $1,198,660 in silver, $687,215 in lead, $147,153 in copper and $1,519,117 in zinc.	• All U.S. railroads were released from federal control Mar. 1. • The CM was officially abandoned—the largest in U.S. history. • The Denver & Rio Grande Western Railroad (D&RGW) was incorporated Nov. 15 by banking interests which owned the Western Pacific Railroad (WP). Five days after the incorporation, the D&RG was sold to the Western Pacific Railroad Corp. (WP).
1921	• The Leadville Mining Development Co. was incorporated Jan. 1 to drive the Canterbury Tunnel from the northwestern slope of Prospect Mountain southeastward to Carbonate Hill. When completed, the tunnel was almost 4,000 feet long and drained many mines on Fryer Hill, Carbonate Hill, in Stray Horse and Evans Gulches.	• On July 27, the new company, the D&RGW, took over operation of the system. • Forty-one miles of D&RGW track had to be repaired after a disastrous flood along the Arkansas River between Canon City and Pueblo destroyed much track. All property and equip-

YEAR	LEADVILLE and COLORADO HISTORY	RAILROAD HISTORY
1921 cont.	No new ore deposits were found, however, and the project was abandoned in the late 1920s. • Lake County mineral production totaled $309,144 in gold, $1,043,497 in silver, $159,205 in lead, $142,841 in copper and only $91,050 in zinc.	ment were in bad condition, due to neglect and mismanagement during and after World War I. • The dismantling of the CM started with the removal of rails between Newcastle and Divide, located near the summit of Ute Pass.
1922	• Another project to drain mines was started by the Leadville Deep Mines Co. Mines at the northern end of Graham Park and Stray Horse Gulch were drained by steam-driven pumps. This project was quite productive until 1931, when all known ore deposits were exhausted. • During the 1920s, the largest industry in Leadville was producing bootleg liquor. Stills were in old mines and buildings. Much lawlessness resulted from such activities. • Lake County mineral production totalcd $413,058 in gold, only $952,048 in silver, $303,700 in lead, $117,635 in copper and $513,171 in zinc.	• D&RGW was forced back into receivership due to a depression, the terrible condition of all equipment, and the 1921 flood. • Despite receivership, the track between Salida and Malta (partly on abandoned CM grade) was rebuilt in several places to reduce curves. • C&S track between Schwanders (south of Buena Vista) and Garos in South Park was removed. It had not been used since 1910. • The CM was legally dissolved and track from Divide to Colorado Springs (via Ute Pass) was sold to the Midland Terminal Railway (MT). This allowed the MT a through route from Cripple Creek to Colorado Springs. The CM route between Arkansas Junction and Basalt was turned into Colorado Highway 104 and the Busk-Ivanhoe Tunnel was used for automobile travel.
1923	• Lake County mineral production totaled $271,504 in gold, $537,787 in silver, $393,747 in lead, $75,321 in copper and $640,220 in zinc. After 1923, the U. S. Bureau of Mines changed its methods of reporting mineral production, combining the value of gold, silver, lead, copper and zinc for yearly totals. • From 1923 to 1930 the Leadville population remained stable at about 4,900.	• C&S rails between Parlin and Gunnison and between Quartz and Hancock were sold. • D&RGW applied to the ICC to abandon the Blue River Branch between Leadville and Dillon Oct. 3 and approval was received Dec. 1.

YEAR	LEADVILLE and COLORADO HISTORY	RAILROAD HISTORY
1924	• Molybdenum began to be used in the automobile industry to harden steel. • Climax Mine opened in September after being closed since 1919. • The 50 active mines in the district produced ores worth $2,716,711. • Public Service Company of Colorado took over operation of the Leadville Light Co.	• D&RGW track between Leadville and Dillon was removed. All traffic across Fremont Pass was now handled by the C&S. • D&RGW receivership ended (again) Oct. 29. • C&S track between Buena Vista and Hancock was abandoned.
1925	• Fifty-two working mines in the Leadville district produced ores worth $2,862,625. • Mines in Graham Park and on Carbonate Hill were drained and back in production for the first time since 1918 and 1919. • Climax molybdenum mine production continued to increase.	• The D&RGW removed the third rail between Salida and Leadville, further isolating the narrow gauge C&S between Buena Vista and Hancock.
1926	• Total production from Leadville mines reached $4,104,615.	• The dismantling of the C&S track between Buena Vista and Romley was completed by Nov. 15.
1927	• Total metallic minerals produced from Leadville district was $2,874,116. • Production of ore at the Climax mine increased to 1,000 tons per day.	• Long-delayed maintenance was finally started by the D&RGW, leaving the company with only a small profit at the end of the year.
1928		• D&RGW traffic increased to the point the Tennessee Pass route was placed under centralized traffic control—the first such installation west of the Mississippi River and one of the first in the United States. • C&S again petitioned the ICC to abandon the 185 miles of track beyond Waterton. Decreased mining revenues, new highways and more automobile traffic reduced the need for the narrow gauge. The company did little to keep the system in good operating condition or obtain larger engines which could pull heavier loads.

YEAR	LEADVILLE and COLORADO HISTORY	RAILROAD HISTORY
1929	• Stock market crashed in October, plunging the country into a depression. • Lake County produced 121,415 tons of gold, silver, lead, zinc and copper ore worth $2,826,261. • The A.V. Smelter reworked slag from the American, Bi-Metallic and Union Smelters. • Molybdenum mining was by shrinkage-slope and caving methods.	
1930	• Notwithstanding hard times, Harrison Ave. was finally paved. • The Leadville Deep Mines Co. continued to develop mines on Carbonate Hill and in Graham Park. • Total mineral production in Lake County was $2,161,628.	• The ICC again denied the C&S's petition to abandon its track. Income was drastically reduced because of the 1929 financial crash, but some badly needed maintenance was undertaken.
1931	• Price of metals dropped so low the Leadville Deep Mining Co. was forced to close. Gold was the only metal worth mining. • Only 26 mines in Lake County operated during the year, producing $458,884.	• C&S track between Black Hawk and Central City was abandoned. Passenger service to Leadville was made tri-weekly with a baggage-mail combine and a coach. The C&S again considered abandoning the line between Como and Leadville.
1932	• Mining production was so low that the Arkansas Valley Smelter operated only part time. • Total Lake County mineral production was $142,759. • Gold came from the Ibex (No. 32-36), Tribune (No. 83) and Venir Mines.	
1933	• Prohibition amendment was repealed and Leadville held a mock funeral for "Mr. Eighteenth Amendment." • The New Deal started a plan to purchase gold and the price was raised from $20 per ounce to $35 per ounce. • This brought out-of-work miners back to California Gulch to again search for the elusive element.	• The Morrison Branch of the old South Park, now C&S, was removed.

YEAR	LEADVILLE and COLORADO HISTORY	RAILROAD HISTORY
1933 cont.	• The Ibex Mine upgraded its operations and by 1937 was the largest shipper to the Arkansas Valley Smelter.	
1934		• D&RGW scrapped the Pitkin Branch from Parlin to Quartz.
1935	• On Mar. 7, Baby Doe Tabor was found dead in a shack at the Matchless Mine where she had lived for many years. • A.V. Smelter operated one furnace throughout the year. • Total Lake County mineral production increased to $377,341. • The Hector Placer in Buckeye Gulch operated from June until October. • Leadville population dropped to 3,771 residents.	• C&S filed another petition Aug. 16 to abandon 116 miles from Waterton to Climax and from Como to Garo, Alma and Leavick. The 14 miles from Climax to Leadville was not included because production of molybdenum at the Climax mine continued to increase each year. • Heavy snows during winter of 1935-36 forced C&S to use the rotary snowplow in Tenmile Canyon and on the High Line.
1936		• C&S delivered a large supply of building material to Climax before the approval to abandon the line was obtained. • The C&S also began dismantling the track between Idaho Springs and Silver Plume; the Georgetown Loop bridge was removed in June.
1937	• The A.V. Smelter operated throughout the year. • Mining through the Yak Tunnel and in the Resurrection Mine continued. • Ibex Mine was the district's largest producer of gold and silver. • Some placer mining continued in California Gulch.	• The last C&S passenger train left Leadville for Denver Apr. 4. After the abandonment of the rest of the line, concentrates from Climax were transferred from narrow gauge to standard gauge D&RGW cars in Leadville. • The C&S left engines 74, 75 and 76, 2 combines, 2 cabooses, rotary, flanger, 57 boxcars, 26 coal cars, 2 reefers and 12 flatcars in Leadville for use on the High Line. • The dual gauge C&S track to mines east of Leadville and in Graham Park area, and the track south of the C&S station south were abandoned.

These photos show Climax before open pit mining began. They were made on an 8x10 negative by Otto Roach of Denver in the summer of 1935 or 1936. In the top photo, the old workings at the Leal Level, built on Charles Senter's original claim, are at left center. The larger group of buildings, at the White Level, are the dorms, boarding house, dining room, crusher plant and tram. The lower view shows the old town of Climax. At this date, the C&S was in service to Denver. In the right center an engine is switching a cut of cars. In the lower center, men are lined up at the company office, perhaps hoping to find work. *(Both photos courtesy Climax Molybdenum Co.)*

YEAR	LEADVILLE and COLORADO HISTORY	RAILROAD HISTORY
1938	• Seventy mines produced $1,237,323 in revenue. • Resurrection Mining Company formed. • Climax increased molybdenum production to 12,000 tons of ore per day. • Resurrection Mine was the largest operation in the district, while some placer gold continued to be recovered in California and Buckeye Gulches.	• Dismantling the C&S mainline between Leadville and Waterton, via Trout Creek Pass, started in May. • C&S management began to think about converting the High Line between Climax and Leadville to standard gauge.
1939	• World War II started in Europe. The prices of metals started to rise.	• Dismantling of the C&S track between Idaho Springs and Silver Plume was completed.
1940		• The isolated C&S branch between Climax and Leadville quit handling ore shipments to the Arkansas Valley Smelter. • D&RGW discontinued passenger service to Leadville and some track in California Gulch was removed. • The D&RGW cutoff between Leadville and Leadville Junction was abandoned.
1941	• The Hamm Mill, built in 1937, operated throughout the 1940s smelting ore from tailing piles and mine dumps, including the Ibex. Tailing piles are the waste left after mills crushed and processed the ore. • Yak Mining, Milling and Tunnel Company dissolved when they deeded their properties to the Resurrection Mining Co. • Japan attacked the U.S. at Pearl Harbor, Dec. 7. U.S. entered World War II.	• C&S track between Golden, Idaho Springs and Black Hawk was abandoned and the rails were all removed by July. • D&RGW track to Graham Park, Wolftone, North Moyer (No. 58) and in California Gulch was removed because many mines had closed.
1942	• U.S. Army began training the Tenth Mountain Division in winter warfare at Camp Hale near Pando, a station on the D&RGW 7 miles north of Tennessee Pass. After the war, Camp Hale's ski area at Cooper Hill was deeded to the city of Leadville. • Lake County Courthouse burned.	• On Oct. 15, C&S received ICC permission to abandon the C&S track between Chatfield and Denver and by Dec. 5 all rail was removed.

Photo stop at Birds Eye Aug 25, 1943 on the final run of a narrow gauge steam train on the High Line. To mark the occasion, officials of Climax Molybdenum Co., the C&S, CB&Q, the U.S. Army and members of the press were invited to a noon banquet at Climax before boarding the train to Leadville. Photographers, including one from Life Magazine, rode on a motor car ahead of the train. Frequent stops were made to record the passing of this era of narrow gauge railroading. The work equipment parked on the siding housed workers who had just completed the job of widening the route. Standard gauge rails are all in place.

(Photo courtesy Climax Molybdenum Co.; Train orders courtesy Alexis McKinney)

YEAR	LEADVILLE and COLORADO HISTORY	RAILROAD HISTORY
1942 cont.	• Construction started on a flotation mill at the portal of the Yak Tunnel in California Gulch. • Resurrection Mining Co. started mining in Resurrection #2 and the White Cap-Cord areas. • Wartime demands for lead and zinc prompted the U.S. Bureau of Mines to rework mine dumps in the district to recover those elements.	
1943	• The U.S. Government financed another drainage tunnel, near the earlier Canterbury Tunnel, to drain the northern end of Leadville Mining District. • Drilling was stopped in 1952 because it was not deep enough to drain the deep workings of many mines. The Yak Tunnel remained the only drainage tunnel that was successful. • During World War II, and later, the Korean War, most production in the Leadville District was from the Ibex and Resurrection Mines, both drained by the Yak Tunnel. • The Ore & Chemical Co. completed a 1,000-ton mill to treat old dump materials.	• The High Line between Climax and Leadville was converted to standard gauge and the last narrow gauge steam train from Climax was Aug. 25 (p. 107). • Old C&S freight cars were dismantled in the Leadville yards and their castings salvaged for rebuilding into flat cars needed by the government for the war effort. Other narrow gauge equipment was shipped to Alaska and Pearl Harbor. • The Busk-Ivanhoe Tunnel was closed to automobile traffic and used only for water diversion.
1944		• D&RGW Ibex and Chrysolite branches were abandoned and track removed. Precious metal mining was curtailed during World War II and rails from these branches were needed elsewhere.
1945		• A new and longer tunnel replaced the original D&RGW Tennessee Pass tunnel. • A cave-in closed the Busk-Ivanhoe (now Carlton automobile) tunnel.
1948	• Climax was the leading U.S. producer of molybdenum.	• D&RGW started to abandon narrow gauge lines all over the state.

YEAR	LEADVILLE and COLORADO HISTORY	RAILROAD HISTORY
1948 cont.	• Resurrection Mine worked on 6 levels from a 1,323-foot-deep vertical shaft and also from the 4-mile Yak Tunnel.	
1951	• City of Leadville started construction of a new sewer system. • Climax mine was worked mostly from long adits, caving, and open pit. • Resurrection Mine still the main gold producer. • During the 1950s, the population of Leadville remained at about 4,200.	• RGS completely abandoned between Durango and Ridgway.
1952	• Construction of two new schools started.	
1953	• Climax Mine became the world's leading molybdenum producer.	
1954	• St. Vincent's Hospital, which had been completed in 1901, was condemned. A new hospital was completed in 1958.	
1955	• A new courthouse was completed. • The price of gold still $35 per ounce. • The Leadville District produced 5,149 fine ounces of gold worth $108,215.	• D&RGW abandoned Marshall Pass route to Gunnison.
1957	• This was the first year Leadville Mining District was not listed in the U.S. Bureau of Mines Yearbook. • Last year of operation for the No. 2 Shaft of the Resurrection Mine. All mining was done through the Yak Tunnel.	• All mainline D&RGW track now controlled by automatic block signals. • Wood in Carlton Tunnel was removed, the tunnel partly retimbered and a concrete water pipe line installed.
1960	• Climax Mine closed their company town and all miners moved to Leadville. • New housing development started in the northwestern part of the city. • Climax, one of the world's largest mining operations, worked on two levels by large-scale caving methods.	• Heavy snows forced C&S to run the converted narrow gauge rotary snowplow on the High Line for the first time since 1957.

YEAR	LEADVILLE and COLORADO HISTORY	RAILROAD HISTORY
1961	• Arkansas Valley Smelter closed. All buildings and equipment sold for scrap.	• Last full year of steam operation on the High Line. This was also the last regular use of steam power on a Class I U.S. railroad.
1962	• A miners' strike at Climax mine started in July and lasted until January 1963. • During late 1960s, a joint venture of American Smelting and Refining Co. and Asarco Mining Co. and the Resurrection Mining Co. reopened the Resurrection Mine. • Construction of the Fryingpan-Arkansas trans-mountain water diversion project was authorized. Water from the Fryingpan and Roaring Fork Rivers on the west slope to be diverted for use by town on the eastern plains. Construction was completed in 1983.	• The last run to Climax for steam engine 641 was Sept. 12. • An SD-9 diesel-electric No. 828, fitted with a snowplow, replaced engine 641 which was retired and donated to the City of Leadville. • In February, the ICC was petitioned to merge the properties of the GN, NP and CB&Q into one system.
1963	• U. S. gold production was at the lowest level in more than 100 years. • No production figures listed for Leadville Mining District. • Construction began on the Frying Pan-Arkansas reclamation project.	• The remainder of the D&RGW branch in California Gulch was removed.
1966	• Kokomo now completely abandoned. Some time later, tailings from Climax molybdenum mine began to cover all signs of the mining camp. The Kokomo post office had closed in 1965.	
1967	• The Leadville campus of Colorado Mountain College opened.	
1970	• Shaft of the Black Cloud mine, located in the cirque at the head of Iowa Gulch completed to a depth of 1655 feet.	• Merger between the GN, NP and CB&Q (owner of C&S) consolidated all holdings to form the Burlington Northern Railroad (BN). The C&S continued to operate as a subsidiary of the BN.

YEAR	LEADVILLE and COLORADO HISTORY	RAILROAD HISTORY
1973	• Open pit mining at Climax started. • New middle school started and completed the following year.	• Reconstruction of the CC Georgetown Loop between Silver Plume and Georgetown was started by the Colorado Historical Society with labor and technical assistance from the U.S. Navy Seabees and a private corporation.
1982	• Climax Mine worked only 194 days because of a worldwide drop in demand for molybdenum. The price was reduced because of large stock piles on hand.	• With massive layoffs at Amax Climax mine, the BN shut down the C&S Climax to Leadville High Line.
1984		• After 2 years of construction, the Devil's Gate high bridge of the Georgetown Loop was dedicated on Aug. 1, which is also "Colorado Day," a State holiday that commemorates the signing of the State Constitution.
1985		• Leadville Historical Society considered taking over the BN Climax branch to operate tourist trains.
1986	• Climax molybdenum production at lowest level in many years. • Leadville picked as the site for the National Mining Museum. • In May, Leadville was designated a National Historic District. • New water treatment plant completed. • Yak Tunnel declared an EPA superfund site for cleanup.	• Last run of a C&S train to Climax was in October.
1987	• Leadville Corporation began to develop mining facilities at the Diamond Shaft of its Resurrection Mine. • The Climax Mine closed Mar. 10. Only maintenance and security crews remained on the payroll.	• The BN sold the 14-mile Leadville-Climax High Line to Stephanie and Kenneth Olsen of Leadville for $10 (p. 17).

On a cold December 1987 morning the rolling stock for the new Leadville, Colorado & Southern Railroad are pulled up the hill from Malta by the D&RGW.

In one of the last movements the D&RGW ever made onto the old C&S property, engines 1918 and 1714 are switched out onto the LC&S track by D&RGW crews.
(Both photos, courtesy, LC&S Railroad)

Forlorn and boarded up, the former C&S depot, waits for spring and the return of passenger traffic to the High Line for the first time in 50 years.

Early spring 1988 found track crews at work relaying the loading track prior to opening day.   *(Both photos, courtesy, LC&S Railroad)*

YEAR	LEADVILLE and COLORADO HISTORY	RAILROAD HISTORY
1988	• Climax Molybdenum Co. added employees at its Henderson Mine and mill and at the Climax Mine. Colorado ranked first in molybdenum production for the nation. • Unique child care center started. Many former miners now worked at ski areas and commuted to work.	• The first run of the new Leadville, Colorado & Southern Railroad (LC&S) was on Memorial Day and uninterrupted service continued until late September. Coaches were constructed on flatcars; seats were obtained from the Regional Transportation District in Denver.
1989	• Colorado ranked 11th of 25 metal-producing States, accounting for slightly more than 2% of the nation's total metals value.	LEADVILLE, COLORADO & SOUTHERN RAILROAD COMPANY
1990	• Organ at First Presbyterian Church was restored and a 100th anniversary concert was held Nov. 11. The organ required manual pumping of bellows until 1936 when an electric wind pump was installed. • Mining continues at the Black Cloud mine which connects with the Irene mine, No. 37, and also with the Yak Tunnel. • According to U.S. Census data, Lake Co. population was 8,850 in 1980 but had dropped to 6,007 by 1990.	

RISCHE, HOOK, AND THE LITTLE PITTSBURG MINE

Among the many prospectors and miners who arrived in Leadville during the spring of 1878, August Rische and George Theodore Hook are legendary for their discovery of the Little Pittsburg mine on Fryer Hill. Their discovery started the biggest boom in Leadville and made many men rich and famous.

Little is known of George Hook except that he was born in Baden, Germany, and came to United States with his parents who settled in the Pittsburgh, Penn. area. It is known that he was in Denver in 1876 and worked as a shoemaker. The circumstances that brought the two men together are unknown but the results of their partnership are notable. In September 1878, after the money started to roll in, Hook decided mining was not for him and he sold his share of the partnership to Rische and Horace Tabor. He was never involved in any more mining ventures. Some accounts say he returned to Pittsburgh, while others report he bought a farm on the plains and died a wealthy man.

Much more is known of August Rische, who was born in Minden, Germany, Nov.17, 1833 and came to this country in 1852. He settled in St. Louis and worked as a shoemaker. Rische enlisted in the army April 26, 1861 and served a 3-month tour of duty with the 4th Regiment, Missouri Volunteer Infantry. After his honorable discharge August 14, 1861, he re-enlisted and served 3 years with Company G, 12th Regiment Missouri Volunteer Infantry. He saw action at the battle of Pea Ridge and was wounded at Vicksburg, Miss., May 22, 1863. He received an honorable discharge from the U.S. Army Sept. 5, 1864 as a sergeant.

August Rische, between 1897 and 1901.
(Collection of Charles W. Rische)

George Theodore Hook.
(Colorado Historical Society)

After the war he came to Colorado, opened a shoemaker's shop in Fairplay and started prospecting. In the fall of 1874 Rische moved to Leadville and worked in the Printer Boy and the Five Twenty mines where he learned the fundamentals of mining.

In April 1878 Rische and Hook approached store owner Horace Tabor for a grubstake and promised Tabor one-third of any discoveries they made. According to Rische's grandson, Charles W. Rische of Denver, the story of the discovery differs somewhat from published accounts. The following circumstances were related to him by his father, August Rische Jr.

After Rische and Hook received a second grubstake of food, mining equipment and jug of whiskey, they hiked back up Fryer Hill near where George H. Fryer had struck rich silver ore a few weeks earlier. After their tramp, and with dusk approaching, it seemed appropriate to rest and sample Tabor's whiskey. One drink led to another and soon it was dark. The two men talked about where to sink a shaft. Finally Rische announced he would throw his hat in the air and they would dig where it landed. Work started the next morning. After spending several weeks sinking a narrow shaft, Rische and Hook struck a rich vein of silver at 27 or 28 feet. Most accounts give the date as May 1.

The Little Pittsburg strike was the dynamite cap that exploded the Leadville boom. The first ore assayed 200 ounces of silver to the ton. By July, the ever-deepening mine was shipping 75 tons of ore per week. The mine was named for Hook's home town of Pittsburgh, Penn. Somehow the "h" was left off when the claim was recorded. According to Duane Smith (1989) in his excellent biography of Horace Tabor, would-be buyers made many attempts to purchase the mine from the three owners. To protect the Little Pittsburg, Tabor, Rische and Hook applied for a Federal mining patent.

Soon the partnership found themselves in court defending themselves against accusations by the owners of the nearby Winnemuck mine that the Little Pittsburg was partly located on their property and that Rische and Hook were mining their ore. This was a common source of litigation because staking out claims and recording them was far from an exact science. Hook soon became disenchanted with the mining and financial problems, and in late September 1878, he sold his interest in the Little Pittsburg to Tabor and Rische for $90,000. Rische and Tabor also purchased his share of the Dives, a small claim next to the Little Pittsburg. Next, the new partners purchased the nearby New Discovery mine from Senator Jerome Chaffee for $125,000. Chaffee had recently purchased Fryer's share of the New Discovery for $50,000! Later that year, Chaffee regretted selling his interest in the New Discovery and persuaded Rische to sell his interest in the Little Pittsburg, Dives and New Discovery for $265,000.

Chaffee and Tabor were able to resolve the dispute between the Little Pittsburg and Winnemuck mines by forming a new company, the Little Pittsburg Consolidated Mining Co. This company then purchased 27 percent of the minority shares of the Winnemuck mine. Such stock and financial manipulations were—and still are—common ways to gain control of a company. Such maneuvers were repeated over and over as Leadville continued to boom. This crisis passed. Tabor and Chaffee continued to grow richer every day. By mid-November 1878, it was estimated that the Little Pittsburg had produced $375,000 and that only $100,000 had been spent to develop the mine. Soon David Moffat was involved in the company, and the three partners continued their meteoric rise to wealth, power and influence. Additional details of Tabor's later life are outlined in the Timeline, p. 60.

During that momentous year of 1878, Tabor expanded his horizons from storekeeping to banking and organized the Bank of Leadville. He was president, friend August Rische was named vice president, and Tabor's son, Maxey, was on the board of directors. George R. Fisher, cashier, actually ran the bank, while the other men simply enjoyed their new titles.

View west of Fryer Hill and the Little Pittsburg Mine in the middle foreground.
(W. H. Jackson, Colorado Historic Society)

On August 5,1879, August Rische married Minna Iunghuhn of Chicago. From this union, August Jr. was born in 1880 and Georgia in 1884. A third child died in infancy. In 1881 the couple built a fine home at Malta. According to a certificate issued by the Soldiers and Sailors Historical and Benevolent Society, Rische served as mayor of Malta and also as a Lake County commissioner. He continued to invest heavily in mining ventures including several mines in the San Juans. For many years he owned a one-fourth interest in the New York mine. He hung on to this mine for many years, always hoping that it would become another Little Pittsburg.

The Rische family moved to Denver sometime before 1884 and purchased a home on the corner of 26th and Stout Streets. Reportedly, he had an elaborate home at East Colfax and Sherman Streets where the State office building is now located. Soon afterward, the family moved to north Denver and built a home at 1659 Boulder Street. He made real estate investments in Denver and was reported to be worth at least $500,000. When the Panic of 1893 hit, the fortune Rische had amassed dwindled to nothing.

View northward of Fryer Hill. Prospect Mtn. is on the skyline. In addition to the mines, there were many substantial houses in this busy Leadville suburb in about 1880.
(W. H. Jackson, Colorado Historic Society)

The following article, in the possession of Rische's grandson, is from an undated, unknown newspaper. The publication date was probably 1899, when Colorado was buried under huge amounts of snow and running a mountain railroad was almost impossible. The article also offers a graphic picture of mining in the wintertime.

FACE OF COUNTRY CHANGED
Snow of Park County Obliterates Hills and Ravines.

August Rische, who has been operating the New York mine near the summit of Mosquito Pass, Park county, came down last Friday. He says that he has been in the mountains more or less every winter for more than 30 years and has never seen so much snow and such severe storms as during the past six weeks. He has been working the mine steadily, but has been unable to make any shipments, and has his ore stacked up in the mine waiting for the opening of the roads.

Mr. Rische says that the snow has changed the entire face of the country in that section. "Where we used to see a hill," said he, "it is all level and where there used to be a hole in the ground there is now a hill. The snow at my cabin is 18 feet deep. My son and I started from the mine Wednesday morning on snowshoes, expecting to catch the train at Alma. We made the station all right about noon, but no train was there and a little later word came that it was stuck in the snow on the other side of Fairplay, and would probably start toward evening. We then walked to Fairplay and took the train, but did not get started until the next morning. We got within a short distance of Como that day when we were again stuck in a drift, and walked to Como where we staid [sic] all night and got started again toward noon Friday, reaching here Friday afternoon.

In later years, August Rische spent most of his summers mining and prospecting with his son, and his winters in Denver with his family. Three years before his death, his friend David Moffat procured a job for him as watchman at the State capitol building in Denver. Rische died May 12, 1910 of pneumonia at the age of 76. His widow lived in Denver until her death in 1936 at the age of 82.

GEOLOGY

ORE DEPOSITS OF THE LEADVILLE MINING DISTRICT[†]

In the late 1850s, when the first optimistic prospectors started panning for gold along the upper reaches of the Arkansas River and its tributary streams, they did not imagine the wealth that lay just a few feet beneath the surface. Between 1859 and 1924, $425,784,550 in gold, silver, lead, copper and zinc were mined from the Leadville District. From 1859 to the late 1980s, more than $800,000,000 in gold, silver, lead, copper, zinc, iron, **manganese** and **bismuth** were produced. The Leadville Mining District is considered to be a "world class" deposit. These figures do not include the production of **molybdenite** from the world's largest **molybdenum** mine at Climax.

This fabulous mineral bounty made Leadville at one time the largest mining town in Colorado. The rich mineral deposits are associated with the Colorado Mineral Belt, a broad belt of northeast-southwest trending zone of Late **Cretaceous** and **Tertiary igneous** rocks. This belt extends from the Colorado Front Range, near Allenspark, southwestward toward the San Juan Mountains. In the Leadville area, the Mineral Belt crosses **Precambrian metamorphic gneisses** and **schists** and igneous **granites** which have been overlain by about 3,000 feet of **Paleozoic** rocks which dip to the east from 12° to 30°. These rocks are broken by a complex series of **faults**, associated with the **uplift** of the Mosquito Range. These faults extend westward to the Arkansas River Valley where they are connected with the Rio Grande **rift** zone. In Colorado, the rift zone extends from the San Luis Valley northward across Poncha Pass and up the Arkansas River almost to Leadville.

Faulting during the Tertiary Period displaced of many of the eastward-dipping **sedimentary** rocks. Major faults trend north-south and are **upthrown** on the east. This brings the eastward-dipping, ore-rich sedimentary rocks to the surface in a series of stairsteps. Faulting also brought ore deposits close to the surface at many places, and made it possible for the earliest **lode** mining to be accomplished with little effort or knowledge of the geology of the area. Because of the extensive faulting, many ore deposits were exposed to **oxidation** and **erosion**.

According to Ogden Tweto (1968), all the Tertiary igneous rocks are older than the ore deposits and nearly all the faults originated before the ore. Many faults were reactivated after mineralization. Ore deposits formed when fluids, released from a **magmatic** source deep within the earth, were deposited in the faults, **veins**, **dikes** and **sills.** These deposits are classified into three groups: (1) silicate-oxide deposits, (2) mixed sulfide veins, and (3) mixed sulfide replacement deposits. US Geological Survey geologists A. H. Koschmann and M.H. Bergendahl published an excellent summary of the ore deposits of the Leadville District in professional paper No. 610, *Principal Gold-producing Districts of the United States* (1968). The following paragraphs are quoted directly from that publication.

> **The silicate-oxide deposits are of little economic value; only small amounts were mined in the early days for smelter flux. These deposits are mixtures of magnetite and hematite in a gangue consisting mainly of serpentine, and are replacement deposits in dolomite. The only ore mined has come from pyritic gold veins that cut these deposits and enriched the adjacent wallrocks.**

[†]Terms in **bold-face** type are defined in the Glossary, p. 123.

The mixed sulfide veins occur mainly in siliceous sedimentary rocks which predominate in the eastern part of the district, where numerous sill-like bodies of porphyry intrude the grit and shale of Pennsylvanian age near the Breece Hill porphyry stock. The largest veins have been productive to a depth of about 1,300 feet below the surface. Some veins are too small to mine but expand into small replacement bodies where they cut dolomite. The veins that cut siliceous sedimentary rocks consist mainly of pyrite with a little interstitial chalcopyrite in a gangue of quartz. Where they grade into replacement deposits, pyrite and quartz persist for a short distance laterally but grade into a mixture of sphalerite and galena in dense quartz or jasperoid. The veins and the pyritic parts of the replacement deposits have been valuable mainly for gold, some of which is primary but much of which has resulted from enrichment in the secondary sulfide zone. The gold is accompanied by some silver and locally by copper.

Replacement deposits of sulfides in dolomite are common in the western part of the district. These replacement bodies lie along fractures or sheeted zones, known locally as contacts, beneath impervious covers such as sills. The largest replacement bodies are at the top of the Leadville Dolomite (Mississippian), and some are more than 2,000 feet long, 800 feet wide, and 200 feet thick.

The mixed sulfide replacement bodies consist of sphalerite and galena with pyrite. The ore contains a few ounces of silver and 0.03 to 0.05 ounce of gold to the ton, but here and there small shoots have been found that are unusually rich in silver and gold and also contain bismuth. Intergrowths of argentite, bismuthinite, and a little galena have been found in this rich ore and also in veins cutting large bodies of the mixed sulfide ore. Tetrahedrite, chalcopyrite, and arsenopyrite also occur locally.

Oxidation and supergene enrichment of the various types of hypogene sulfides produced ore of variable mineralogy. Some of the ores are rich in cerussite and cerargyite; others, in smithsonite and hemimorphite, manganese-iron-bismuth oxides, chalcocite-covellite-gold-silver, and argentite-silver. Much of the coarse gold in the placers of California Gulch is believed to be of reworked supergene origin.

The slopes of the Mosquito Range east of Leadville collect large amounts of snow during the long winter months. Meltwater percolates downward along exposed layers of sedimentary rock and along faults, and then flows into mine workings. The ease with which water moves through the rocks and collects in mine shafts has caused serious problems for miners through the years. This led to the construction of extensive and very expensive drainage tunnels, including the Yak, Leadville, and Canterbury. The water also causes **alteration** of the rocks and metallic minerals.

ALPINE GLACIATION

About 2.4 million years ago the climate, worldwide, became much cooler and snow began to accumulate to great depths around both the north and south poles. Throughout the Colorado mountains during the **Ice Ages**, many mountain valleys were periodically filled with large accumulations of snow that compacted into slow-moving rivers of ice, called **alpine glaciers**. These glaciers carved and sculptured the mountain peaks into dramatic, sharp, pointed horns and scooped out spectacular bowl-shaped amphitheaters (**cirques**) along the highest parts of the mountain ranges. The Mosquito Range, east of Leadville, and the Sawatch Range, across the Arkansas River Valley to the west, were extensively glaciated.

Glacial debris at M.P. 142.5.
(Frank W. Osterwald)

Geologic sill opposite M.P. 148.0.
(Ray W. Osterwald)

View west near MP 148.5. Mt. Massive is on the skyline. Along both sides of the East Fork of the Arkansas River glacial moraines are outlined by the evergreen forest.
(Frank W. Osterwald)

GENERALIZED STRATIGRAPHIC SECTION OF LAKE COUNTY

Era	Period	Formation	Thickness in feet	Formation Description
Cenozoic	Quarternary		0-500	Alluvium, terrace, outwash, pediment silts, sands, and gravels, glacier deposits, landslide debris, and rock glacier deposits.
	Tertiary		0-6,000	Siltstones, sandstones, conglomerates, and volcanic ash and tuff beds. Middle and Lower Tertiary and Upper Cretaceous ore-bearing igneous rocks emplaced during a time of mountain building (Laramide Orogeny). Igneous rhyolite porphyry, quartz monzonite, grandiorite and quartz diorite were intruded into older sedimentary rocks as stock, dikes, sills and irregular bodies.
Mesozoic	Upper Cretaceous	Pierre Shale	2,000	Dark-gray shale with interbedded sand- and siltstones.
	Lower Cretaceous	Dakota Sandstone	150-160	Light-gray and tan sandstone and conglomerates with minor shale or shaly sandstones.
	Upper Jurassic	Morrison Formation	250	Interbedded light-gray sandstone, and gray limestone.
		Entrada Sandstone	60	Gray to brownish-red sandstone.
Paleozoic	Lower Permian, Upper to Middle Pennsylvanian	Maroon Formation	1,700-4,200	Maroon and grayish-red sandstone, conglomerate, and mudstone.
	Middle Pennsylvanian	Minturn Formation	1,000-6,300	Gray, pale-yellow, and red sandstone, conglomerate, shale, with some limestone.
		Belden Formation	0-400	Dark-gray to black shale, limestone, and sandstone. [Unconformity]
	Lower Pennsylvanian	Molas Formation	0-40	Gray, yellow, and brown regolithic silt and clay with chart fragments.
	Lower Mississippian	Leadville Limestone (or Dolomite)	0-190	Gray or bluish-gray limestone or dolomite. [Unconformity]
	Lower Mississippian and Upper Devonian	Chaffee Group — Gilman Sandstone	0-50	Brown sandstone. [Unconformity]
		Chaffee Group — Dryer Dolomite	0-150	Brown and gray dolomite.
	Lower Devonian	Chaffee Group — Parting Formation	0-65	White, tan, pink quartite and conglomerate; some interbedded-green shale. [Unconformity]
	Middle Ordovician	Harding Sandstone	0-80	Gray and brown quartzite and sandstone, and green shale.
	Lower Ordovician	Manitou Dolomite	0-120	Gray dolomite. [Unconformity]
	Cambrian	Peerless Formation	0-112	Green, brown, red, and buff sandy dolomite, dolomitic sandstone, dolomite, and dolomitic shale.
		Sawatch Quartzite	0-220	White quartzite. [Unconformity]
Proterozoic	Precambrian	Granite, diorite, gneiss, and schist		

Modified from Bryant, *et. al.,* (1988)

Along both sides of the Arkansas River Valley are many signs that ancient glaciers once flowed downward into the valley. The sides of the valleys have been steepened and gouged out by the moving ice. As glacial ice froze to the walls of the mountains, chunks of rock were plucked from the bedrock and carried away by the ice. The loosened rocks carried in the ice also gouged, scraped, polished, and hollowed out the valleys into their present U-shaped cross-sections.

When the climate became warmer about 14,000 years ago and the glaciers started to retreat, they dumped ridges and mounds of rock debris in and along the sides of the valleys. Today these mounds (**moraines**) of loose, rounded **boulders**, **cobbles**, **sand**, **gravel**, **soil** and **silt** stand as stark reminders of the power of moving ice. Much of the LC&S grade is built on glacial debris left by those retreating glaciers. Large **lateral moraines** were deposited along the sides of the Upper Arkansas River Valley.

Unconsolidated stream, **terrace**, and **outwash** deposits of sand, silt and gravel are found on the valley floors. These deposits are younger than the glacial debris and are partly derived from the older glacial deposits. **Landslide** debris and **talus** deposits complete the picture of weathering and erosion to the surface of the land.

GLOSSARY OF GEOLOGIC TERMS

alpine glacier, Any glacier in a mountain range originating in a cirque and flowing down a valley.

alteration, Any change in the mineral composition of a rock brought about by physical or chemical means, especially by the action of hydrothermal solutions.

batholith, A large intrusive igneous mass that is more than 40 square miles in surface exposure and is composed of medium- to coarse-grained rocks. No visible floor of such large rock masses has been reported.

bismuth, A metallic element used in making some alloys needing a low melting point. It is also used in medicine, diagnostic X-rays and cosmetics.

boulder, A detached piece of rock larger than a volleyball.

Cenozoic, An era of geologic time from the beginning of the Tertiary Period (66 million years ago) to the present.

cirque, A steep-walled, scoop-shaped depression high on the side of a mountain caused by headward erosion by an alpine glacier.

cobble, A detached piece of rock, between a tennis ball and a volleyball in size.

columnar joint, Parallel, hexagonal or pentagonal-shaped columns in either intrusive or extrusive rocks that formed as the result of contraction during cooling.

Cretaceous, The final period of the Mesozoic Era that covered the period of time between 144 million and 66 million years ago.

dike, A tabular body of igneous rock filling a fissure in older rocks which it entered as a molten fluid. The fissure cuts across the structure of the older rock.

diorite, An intrusive igneous rock, composed mainly of plagioclase feldspar and one or more ferromagnesian minerals. It usually has a gray or dark-green color and a texture similar to granite.

dolomite, A common rock-forming mineral, $CaMg(CO_3)_2$.

dolomite rock, A sedimentary rock with more than 50 percent, by weight, of the mineral dolomite.

erosion, The general transport process by which rocks and rocky materials of the Earth's crust are moved from one place to another.

extrusive, *adj.* Said of igneous rocks that have been ejected onto the surface of the Earth.

fault (zone), A break or breaks in rock along which movement has taken place.

feldspar, The most common group of minerals, found in nearly all igneous rocks. Feldspars are aluminum silicates having varying amounts of sodium, potassium, or calcium. Alkali (potassium) feldspars include orthoclase and microcline; plagioclase (sodium and calcium) feldspars include albite and anorthosite.

fill, Man-made deposits of soil, sand, gravel or waste materials from mining or dredging.

gangue, The valueless rock or mineral aggregates in an ore.

glacial debris, A mixture of unsorted, unstratified, unconsolidated clay, sand, gravel, cobbles and boulders of varying size and shape.

gneiss, A coarse-textured metamorphic rock with mineral grains that have a layered or banded appearance.

granite, A light-colored igneous rock composed of about 60% potash feldspar and 30% quartz with dark-colored mica and/or hornblende. The rock is usually light-colored and has a granular texture.

gravel, A detached piece of rock about the size of a marble.

Ice Ages, A time of extensive glacial activity which took place during the Pleistocene Epoch, starting about 2.4 million years ago and ending 14,000 years ago.

igneous rock, A rock or mineral that cooled and solidified from molten or partly molten rock material (magma). One of the three main classes of rock.

intrusion, (in igneous rock) The process of emplacement of magma in preexisting rock.

intrusive, *adj.* Of or pertaining to *intrusion*, both the processes and the rock so formed.

landslide, A mass of loosened rocks and/or debris that slides or falls down a hillside or slope.

lateral moraine, A ridge-like deposit of glacial debris along the side of a glacier or glaciated valley.

limestone, A sedimentary rock consisting of at least 95% of the mineral calcite and less than 5% dolomite.

lode claim, A mining claim containing a ore deposit in consolidated rock.

magma, Naturally occurring melted, mobile igneous rock material within the Earth and capable of intrusion and extrusion. When magma flows or pours out onto the Earth's surface, it is called lava.

magmatic, Of, pertaining to, or derived from magma.

manganese, A grayish-white metallic element used with other metals as alloys.

metamorphic rock, One of the three main classes of rocks. Metamorphic rocks are those that have been changed from one form to another by heat, pressure or deep burial within the Earth.

Mesozoic, An era of geologic time from the end of the Paleozoic (about 245 million years ago) to the beginning of the Cenozoic Era (66 million years ago).

molybdenite, A lead-gray to bluish-gray mineral, MoS_2, that is the principal ore of molybdenum.

molybdenum, A soft, silver-white metallic element used in metal alloys.

moraine, A mound or ridge of unsorted, unstratified glacial debris deposited by the direct action of slowly moving glacial ice.

orthoclase feldspar, Potassium-rich feldspar, one of the most common rock-forming minerals. Color varies from white to pink to yellow.

outwash, (glacial geology) Rock debris removed from a glacier by meltwater and laid down by streams downstream from the glacier itself.

oxidation, oxidized zone, An area of mineral deposits modified by surface water alteration.

Paleozoic, An era of geologic time which began at the end of the Precambrian Era (570 million years ago) and ended about 245 million years ago.

phenocryst, A relatively large, conspicuous crystal in a porphyritic rock.

placer claim, Surficial ore deposit formed by the concentration of mineral particles in loose debris.

plug, A vertical, pipe-like body of magma that represents the conduit to a former volcanic vent.

porphyry, An igneous rock with large crystals (phenocrysts) surrounded by finer-grained minerals.

Precambrian, The earliest major subdivision of geologic time, being the elapsed time from the formation of the earth to the beginning of the Cambrian Period about 570 million years ago. The first era of the Earth's history.

pyrite, A common, pale-bronze or brass-yellow mineral, FeS_2. Often called "fool's gold."

quartzite, A very hard, metamorphic sandstone so firmly cemented that breakage occurs through the grains rather than between them. Also a very hard, unmetamorphosed sandstone consisting chiefly of quartz grains that have been cemented together with silica.

Quaternary, The second period of the Cenozoic Era (following the Tertiary), thought to cover the last 2.4 million years.

replacement, The process of practically simultaneous capillary solution and deposition by which a new mineral of partly or wholly differing chemical composition may grow in and replace the body of an old mineral or mineral aggregate.

rhodochrosite, A pink to rose-red or gray-colored manganese carbonate mineral. It is a minor ore manganese.

rhyolite, A light-colored volcanic rock, similar in composition to granite but much finer texture.

rift, A major flaw in the Earth's crust, caused by large forces that thin the Earth's crust by slowly pulling apart a strip, thus allowing the strip to sag. Rifts contain many faults caused by local forces that break the rocks, and drop many blocks downward into the sagging strip.

sand, Rock or mineral particles that are less than 2 mm and more than 1/16 mm in diameter.

schist, A crystalline metamorphic rock with closely spaced foliation (layering) which tends to split easily into thin slabs or flakes. With thicker foliation, the rock grades into gneiss.

sedimentary rock, One of the three main kind of rocks, consisting of sediment that accumulated in layers and has been consolidated into a rock.

sill, An intrusive body of igneous rock that has solidified in horizontal, flattened sheets between and parallel to the bedding planes in stratified rocks.

silt, Fine-grained sediment carried or laid down by rivers or oceans. The word generally applies to unconsolidated material that is smaller in size than sand and larger than clay.

soil, All fine-grained, unconsolidated material that overlies bedrock. Geologically, soil should be capable of supporting plant life.

stock, An igneous intrusive mass of rock that is less than 40 square miles in surface exposure, that resembles a batholith but is smaller in size.

talus, An accumulated heap of rock fragments derived from, and lying at the base, of a cliff or very steep slope.

terrace, Any long, narrow, relatively level or gently sloping surface, bounded along one edge by a steeper descending slope and along the other surface by a steeper ascending slope.

Tertiary Period, The first period of geologic time during the Cenozoic Era. The Tertiary Period was preceded by the Cretaceous Period of the Mesozoic Era and was followed by the Quaternary Period.

unconformity, A break or gap in the geologic record where a rock unit is overlain by another that is not next in stratigraphic succession.

uplift, A structurally high area in the crust, produced by positive movements that raise or upthrust the rocks, as in a dome or arch.

upthrown, *adj.* Rocks on the side of a fault that have moved upward, relative to the other side.

vein, A thin, tabular igneous intrusion into a crevice. Smaller in size than a dike.

wetland, An area in which water is at or near the land surface.

NATURE

LIFE ZONES

Life zones may be defined as communities of plants, mammals and birds that live in specific elevational zones. These zones contain distinctive assemblages of plants and animals that have achieved a balance between local climate and elevation. In Colorado there are six life zones from the plains to the alpine tundra: the *plains* (4,000 ft. to 5,500 ft.), the *Upper Sonoran* (in Western Colorado), the *foothills* (5,500 ft. to 8,000 ft.), *montane* (8,000 ft. to 9,500 ft.), *subalpine* (9,500 ft. to treeline), and the *alpine* life zone, above treeline.

The route of the LC&S is in the subalpine life zone for the entire trip. In central Colorado, this zone extends from about 9,500 ft. to upper treeline, which at this latitude is between 11,500 and 11,600 feet. Engelmann spruce and subalpine fir forests dominate the subalpine zone, but limber pine, lodgepole pine, and aspen forests also grow here.

Many factors, in addition to climate and elevation, affect the growth of plant and animal communities. Soil type, slope conditions, topography, moisture, humidity, wind and temperature also change the balance between climate and elevation. Some plants and animals thrive in wet, moist areas; other prefer dry, sunny slopes. Wind direction and velocity affect plant growth in many ways. Near treeline (commonly called "timberline") the spruces and firs are dwarfed and misshapened by fierce winds and short growing seasons. Changes between zones are easier to observe in the mountains than they are on the plains. This is because you can quickly go from one zone into another by going up or down in elevation.

Major species of trees delineate zonal boundaries; these boundaries are not sharp, but merge and overlap each other. Many plants and animals live in more than one zone.

Within each life zone, various ecosystems comprise specific biological differences. Each ecosystem attracts and supports a wide, but distinct, variety of plants, birds, insects and mammals. Commonly, the north-facing slope of a valley supports a different ecosystem from that found on an opposite south-facing slope.

At least 35 species of mammals make their home in the subalpine spruce-fir forests of Colorado. Mammals that may be found along the LC&S grade include Nuttall's cottontail, snowshoe hare, white-tailed jackrabbit, least chipmunk, yellow-bellied marmot, golden-mantled ground squirrel, porcupine, coyote, possibly a black bear, marten, ermine, long-tailed weasel, striped skunk, bobcat, elk, and mule deer.

IDENTIFYING CONIFERS

Conifers are easy to identify because the leaves (needles) and cones of one genus are different from other genera.

Pines have needles gathered together at the base (in clusters of two to five) bound into little sheaths that commonly wear off after the first year's growth. The cones contain seeds in their thick, overlapping woody scales.

Spruce needles are scattered over the twigs singly, are sharp-pointed and four-sided. When the needles fall from the twigs, they leave roughened surfaces like small vegetable graters. Cones hang downward like pendants and have parchment-like scales.

Yellow Paintbrush

Red Paintbrush

Little Red Elephant

Purple Fringe
(All photos, Doris B. Osterwald)

Marmot

Mule Deer

Coyote

Pika
(All photos, © Chase Swift)

Firs have flat, blunt needles that leave smooth, round scars on the twigs when they fall off. Cones on Douglas firs are numerous and hang like pendants. Subalpine firs have fewer cones, which grow erect and cluster near the tops of the trees.

Junipers have needles that are subdivided into tiny segments resembling scales. These are from 1/2 to 1 inch long and attached closely to twigs. Cones look like small, bluish-colored berries.

KEY TO IDENTIFING CONIFERS

To use the key, start with **1A** and follow the numbers as directed.

1A. If the needles are 1 inch long or longer, and the seeds are in cones, go to----**2**

    B. If the needles look like scales less than 1 inch long, and the seeds are in berries, go to ---**11**

2A. If the needles are in bundles of two to five, go to ----------------------------**3**

    B. If the needles are single, go to --**7**

3A. If the needles are in bundles of two or three, go to -----------------------------**4**

    B. If the needles are in bundles of five, go to ----------------------------------**6**

4A. If the needles are 3 to 6 inches long, mostly in bundles of two or three; cones are 3 to 5 inches long; and the bark is reddish-brown on mature trees, the tree is a ---**PONDEROSA PINE**
(Pinus ponderosa)
Up to 150 ft. tall

    B. If the needles are 3/4 to 3 inches long, mostly in bundles of two, go to--**5**

5. If the needles are yellow-green, in bundles of two, 1-1/2 to 3 inches long; the tree is tall and slender with thin bark; cones are 1-1/2 to 3 inches long that remain on the branches for years without opening or dropping their seeds, the tree is a ---**LODGEPOLE PINE**
(Pinus contorta **var.** *latifolia)*
Up to 100 ft. tall

6. If the needles are in bundles of five, from 1-1/2 to 3 inches long, slender, long-pointed, not toothed; the cones are from 4 to 10 inches long and do not have bristles; the bark is smooth and silvery gray on young trees, grayish black on mature trees, the tree is a --**LIMBER PINE**
(Pinus flexilis)
Up to 80 ft. tall

7A. If the needles are stiff, four-sided, (not rounded) and sharp-pointed, go to ---**8**

B. If the needles are not stiff, flat, nor sharp-pointed, go to ---------------------**9**

8A. If the needles are very stiff, sharp and green to silvery gray-green; the cones are 2-1/2 to 4 inches long; and the tree has dark gray bark, it is a --------------------
COLORADO BLUE SPRUCE
(Picea pungens)
Up to 100 ft. tall

B. If the needles are dark green but not as stiff and sharp as **8A**; the cones are 1 to 3 inches long; and the main trunk is smooth and a clean, cinnamon-brown color, the tree is an ---
ENGELMANN SPRUCE
(Picea engelmannii)
Up to 125 ft. tall

9. If the needles are dark green; the 1-1/2 to 3-inch cones hang down and three-pointed bracts stick out between the cone scales, the tree is a --------------------
DOUGLAS FIR
(Pseudotsuga menziesii)
Up to 100 ft. tall

131

10. If the needles are about 1 inch long and tend to turn upward so the foliage appears flattened on branches; the 3- to 4-inch purplish-brown cones stand up; the grayish-white bark is smooth, the tree is a --------------- **SUBALPINE FIR**

(Abies lasiocarpa)
From 60 to 100 ft. tall

11A. If the conifer is a shrub less than 3 ft. high, has sharp, prickly needles at the ends of the branches and the branches have white lines down them, it is a ---------
DWARF JUNIPER
(Juniperus communis)

A. If the tree is as much as 20 ft. tall, and most of the needles are divided into tiny segments (like scales) and are flattened against the branchlets, it is a ---
ROCKY MOUNTAIN JUNIPER
(Juniperus scopulorum)

COMMON SUBALPINE WILDFLOWERS

The most common wildflowers likely to be seen along the track, are listed below by color and in the order in which they bloom from early summer until frost.

WHITE to CREAM COLOR:

WILD CANDYTUFT—*Thlaspi montanum.*
MARSH MARIGOLD—*Caltha leptosepala.*
GLOBEFLOWER—*Trollius laxus.*
BITTER-CRESS—*Cardamine cordifolia.*
DOTTED SAXIFRAGE—*Saxifraga bronchialis.*
SNOWBALL SAXIFRAGE—*Saxifraga rhomboidea.*
WILD STRAWBERRY—*Fragaria ovalis.*
PUSSYTOES—*Antennaria rosea.*
ALPINE PUSSYTOES—*Antennaria alpina.*
KINNIKINNIK—*Arctostaphylos uva-ursi.*

TWISTED STALK—*Streptopus amplexifolius.*
DEATH CAMAS or WAND LILY—*Zigadenus elegans.*
CURLED LOUSEWORT—*Pedicularis racemosa.*
PARRY LOUSEWORT—*Pedicularis parryi.*
WOOD NYMPH—*Moneses uniflora.*
PEARLY EVERLASTING—*Anaphalis margaritacea.*
ALPINE ANEMONE—*Anemone narcissiflora.*
BISTORT—*Polygonum bistortoides.*

COLORADO THISTLE—*Cirsium coloradense.*
YARROW—*Achillea lanulosa.*
TRAILING or WHIPLASH FLEABANE—*Erigeron flagellaris.*
BLACK-HEADED DAISY—*Erigeron melanocephalus.*

YELLOW and ORANGE:
MONKEYFLOWER—*Mimulus guttatus.*
GLOBEFLOWER—*Trollius laxas.*
SUBALPINE BUTTERCUP—*Ranunculus eschscholtzii.*
LARGE LEAF AVENS—*Geum macrophyllum.*
WALLFLOWER—*Erysimum capitatum.*
GOLDEN BANNER—*Thermopsis divaricarpa.*
TWISTED-POD DRABA—*Draba streptocarpa.*
YELLOW MOUNTAIN PARSLEY—*Pseudocymopterus montanus.*
GLAUCOUS CINQUEFOIL—*Potentilla diversifolia.*
STONECROP—*Sedum lanceolatum.*
HEART-LEAVED ARNICA—*Arnica cordifolia.*
(SENECIOS are also called butterweeds, groundsels or ragworts.)
RAYLESS SENECIO—*Senecio bigelovii.*
TRIANGULAR-LEAVED RAGWORT—*Senecio triangularis.*
BLACK-TIPPED SENECIO—*Senecio atratus*
WOOLY GROUNDSEL—*Senecio canus.*
SULPHUR FLOWER—*Eriogonum umbellatum.*
YELLOW SWEETCLOVER—*Melilotus officinalis.*
BUTTER-AND-EGGS—*Linaria vulgaris.*
YELLOW PAINTBRUSH—*Castilleja occidentalis*
GOLDEN ASTER—*Heterotheca fulcrata*
DWARF GOLDENROD—*Solidago spathulata.*
Macronema discoideum

BLUE and BLUISH PURPLE:
BLUE VIOLET—*Viola adunca.*
TALL CHIMING BELLS—*Mertensia ciliata.*
MOUNTAIN LUPINE—*Lupinus argenteus.*

HAREBELL or BLUEBELL, *Campanula rotundifolia.*
BELLFLOWER—*Campanula parryi.*
EARLY BLUE DAISY—*Erigeron vetensis.*
ALPINE PENSTEMON—*Penstemon alpinus.*
DUSKY BEARD TONGUE—*Penstemon whippleanus.*
PURPLE FRINGE—*Phacelia sericea*
JACOB'S LADDER—*Polemonium delicatum.*
COLORADO BLUE COLUMBINE—*Aquilegia caerulea.*
SUBALPINE LARKSPUR—*Delphinium barbeyi.*
AMERICAN MONKSHOOD—*Aconitum columbianum.*
BLUE ERIGERON—*Erigeron vertensis*
SUBALPINE DAISY—*Erigeron peregrinus.*
PINNATE-LEAVED DAISY—*Erigeron pinnatisectus.*
ROCKY MOUNTAIN FRINGED GENTIAN—*Gentianopsis thermalis.*
STAR GENTIAN—*Swertia perennis.*
PARRY GENTIAN—*Gentiana calycosa.*

RED, PINK, and REDDISH-PURPLE:
RED ANEMONE—*Anemone multifida* var. *globosa,*
WESTERN RED COLUMBINE—*Aquilegia elegantula.*
MOUNTAIN BLUEBERRY—*Vaccinium myrtillus.*
SHOOTING STAR—*Dodecatheon pulchellum.*
LITTLE RED ELEPHANT—*Pedicularis groenlandica*
KINGS CROWN—*Sedum integrifolium.*
ROSE CROWN—*Sedum rhodanthum.*
TWINFLOWER—*Linnaea borealis.*
SPOTTED CORAL ROOT—*Corallorhiza maculata.*
PUSSYTOES—*Antennaria rosea.*
PARRY PRIMROSE—*Primula parryi.*
ROSY PAINTBRUSH—*Castilleja rhexifolia.*
COMMON WILD GERANIUM—*Geranium caespitosum.*
FIREWEED—*Epilobium angustifolium.*
TANSY ASTER—*Machaeranthera bigelovii.*
LEAFY-BRACT ASTER—*Aster foliaceus.*
SUBALPINE DAISY—*Erigeron peregrinus.*

RAILROADING

ALONG THE HIGH LINE

Few photos of passenger service on the High Line exist, which makes this picture doubly interesting. In an action scene from the early 1930s, the morning train to Denver has backed onto the east leg of the Climax wye to wait for an obviously late westbound freight train. The conductor, on the rear platform, is nervously reaching for his watch, while an engineman walks alongside the train. The freight, pulled by Engine #76, is passing on the mainline while the fireman studies the injector overflow. The other plume of coal smoke is from another locomotive which is cut in near the center of the freight train. (Photo courtesy Climax Molybdenum Co.)

The crew readied train #71 for its eastbound departure for Denver, Feb. 22, 1934. Engine #9's spark arrestor is folded down, as a brush fire is not too likely! The #9 was built in 1884 by the Cooke Locomotive Works as a 29 ton 2-6-0. It was the regular motive power on the train and pulled the last run to Denver. The #9 was displayed by the Burlington Railroad at the 1939-40 New York World's Fair. It returned to Colorado in December 1988 as a gift from Burlington Northern Railroad to the Colorado Historical Society. This engine is now at Silver Plume, Colorado.
(Both photos, Otto C. Perry, Denver Public Library, Western History Dept.)

Coach #73 stands at Leadville on the cold morning of Feb. 22, 1934. Fresh snow has fallen, but a fire in the coal stove will keep the passengers on train #71 warm this frigid winter day. Built in 1896 by the St. Charles Company, the coach was retired in April 1937, three years after this picture was taken.

Baldwin 2-8-0 #73 was filmed the same day, Feb. 22, 1934 in the Leadville yard. The #73 was built for the UPD&G in 1897 as one of 3 new engines which were re-numbered #71, #72 and #73 by the C&S. The #71 is occasionally seen in service at Central City, Colo. Engine #73 survived until October 1940.
(Both photos, Otto C. Perry, Denver Public Library, Western History Dept.)

About 6 weeks after the last runs between Denver and Leadville were made, Mr. Otto Perry found combination car #26 at Leadville, May 16, 1937. This car was built for the DSP&P by the Ohio Falls Co. as car #127, and was rebuilt in 1893 by the UP. The C&S rebuilt it again in 1915. By 1937 it was officially a "tool car" and was in Leadville as late as 1943.   (Otto C. Perry, Denver Public Library, Western History Dept.)

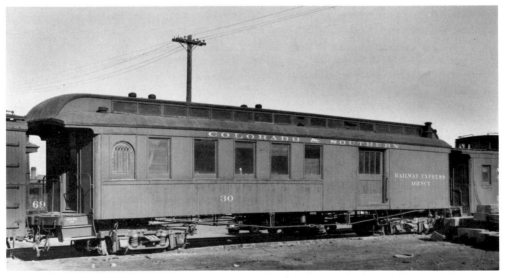

Combination baggage and chair car #30 was stored at Leadville, June 4, 1938. This car, painted dark green with gold lettering, was a real old-timer, being built in 1873 for the DSP&P by the J. G. Brill Co., as car #130. The C&S rebuilt it in 1915, and it was also used as a "tool car" after 1937. Minus trucks, the body was in Leadville in 1959.
(Richard H. Kindig)

The following series of eight photos were taken by Richard H. Kindig June 4, 1938.

Engine #74 gets a ride on the Leadville turntable on the morning of June 4, 1938. Built in April 1898 by the Brooks Locomotive Works as #30 for the Colorado & Northwestern, this locomotive served three other Colorado railroads. The C&NW became the Denver, Boulder & Western in March 1909, serving the mining district west of Boulder. The C&S bought the #74 from a Denver junkyard in February 1921. No. 74 served as a freight engine, and was used on the High Line until August 1943. In 1949, the Rio Grande Southern obtained the engine and used it in the San Juan Mountains until 1951 when the RGS was abandoned. It was saved from the scrapper's torch when the city of Boulder purchased the locomotive. The #74, wearing her original #30, is presently on display in Boulder, Colo.

Fourteen months after regular operation between Denver and Climax ceased, engine #69 was still working the Leadville to Climax Turn. Scrapping the mainline east of Climax began in the summer of 1938. Hostler Diamond (left) and engineer J. B. Oshier (right) have stopped their work while Mr. Kindig records the scene. Engine #69 was built in 1890 by the Baldwin Locomotive Works as #272 for the DL&G. On April 27, 1943, the #69 was shipped to Alaska after being drafted by the U.S. Army for World War II service in Alaska on the White Pass & Yukon Railroad. It was scrapped in 1946 at Seattle Wash.

The crew has taken the #69 into the yard to switch out the consist of the morning's Climax Turn. They are coupling onto a long cut of freight cars.

With the switching chores completed, the crew finishes readying #69 for the Climax Turn.

At 9:34 a.m., the #69 left Leadville with a three-car train for Climax. To the right is the roundhouse and engine #8. In July 1938 the #69 and #71 hauled engine #8 east over Fremont and Boreas Passes to Denver. The #8 was not under steam and never ran again. Through the summer, #69 and #71 were used out of Denver on the remaining operations, and that fall the #71 pulled the last C&S train across South Park.

The Climax Turn is pictured in this distant view at 9:57 a.m. making its way up the hill at MP 141. Soon the crew will have their train at Climax.

The train has gone around the big loop in the valley at the headwaters of the Arkansas River, and is above the old townsite of Alicante at MP 138.5.

About 11 a.m. the #69 arrived at Climax, and is standing at the depot, MP 137.46. Although the mainline stretches ahead of the engine's pilot, the line was officially abandoned and no trains operated east of Climax.

This photograph at Climax is unusual in that the cars in the foreground belong to the D&RG. They would have been interchanged at Leadville in 1925 or before, as the narrow gauge 3rd rail from Salida was removed in 1925. This winter scene also illustrates how the cirque on Bartlett Mtn. looked in the late 1920s or early 1930s before much mining by shrinkage-slope and caving methods was undertaken. By 1991, Ceresco Ridge (on right side above buildings and trees) has been completely removed by mining operations. (Photo courtesy Climax Molybdenum Co.)

By 1938, mining at Climax had grown and daily freight runs were made to the mine from Leadville. This photo of engine #74 was taken April 29, 1939 in the Climax yards. (Otto C. Perry, Denver Public Library, Western History Dept.)

Famous railroad photographer Otto Perry traveled to Leadville (in spite of wartime gasoline rationing!) for a day of train-chasing. On Wednesday, June, 16, 1943, the following photos were taken along the High Line. Two other pictures taken on this same trip are on pages 53 and 55. All photos are from the Denver Public Library, Western History Dept.

This classic early-morning view shows #76, called out as the helper engine, on the service track at Leadville. The #76 was built for the Colorado & Northwestern in June, 1898, as #32. After pulling the last C&S narrow gauge train in August 1943, it was sold for use on the Central Railway of Peru and converted to standard gauge. Rumored to be lying at the bottom of a cliff in the Andes Mountains, its fate after the 1950s is not known.

Having finished servicing the locomotive, the crew members make up the morning train in the Leadville yard. The roof of St. Vincent's Hospital is visible behind the engine.

Otto Perry rode in the caboose on this eastbound trip to Climax. Here, engines #74 and #76 labor up the grade near Dutch Gulch at MP 143.5.

The engines have gotten thirsty bringing their 14-car train from Leadville and have stopped at the French Gulch water tank. Engine #74's fireman is busy on the tender. In a little over two months, scenes such as this will disappear forever with standard gauging of the line.

With all the work at Climax completed, the helper returned to Leadville. Perry caught the engine running light, westbound at Dutch Gulch, MP 143.7.

A few minutes later, engine #74 passed with the westbound train. Perry had walked about 1/2 mile east of MP 143.25 and made this classic photo of the narrow gauge at work on the High Line.

These 4-wheel cabooses trailed narrow gauge trains around Colorado since the 1880s and were "home" to many early DSP&P employees. Prospect Mtn. is on the skyline.

On Nov. 11, 1941, about a month before Pearl Harbor, Perry found the #75 leaving for Climax with seven cars, and he followed the train to Climax. Engine #75 was one of three Brooks 2-8-0's purchased by the C&S in February, 1921 following the abandonment of the Denver, Boulder & Western.

Just west of MP 138, near the site of Wortman, Colo. Hwy. 91 is relatively close to the right-of-way. Perry walked through the snow the short distance to the track and caught the train working the last mile into the Climax yard.

Later the same day, with the switching at the mine completed, the crew heads for Leadville with loads and empties. Otto Perry went back to the same location, MP 138, and photographed the westbound train.

THE ROAD WIDENS

With the standard gauging of the Climax Branch, one era on the High Line ended and another started. For the next 19 years, the C&S used their 600-class 2-8-0s on the Climax Turn. The 600s were built between 1901 and 1907, and were less than ten years newer than the narrow gauge locomotives they replaced! Engine #638, along with the #641, were the last two active C&S steam engines. In 1962, the #638 was retired and given to the City of Trinidad where it is now on display.

(Robert W. Richardson, Colorado Railroad Museum)

WINTER TIME ON THE HIGH LINE

Railroading along the High Line during the winter months offers opportunities for interesting and unusual photographs, as recorded in this and the next four views taken by Dick Kindig, four days after Christmas 1959. Here, engine #641 backs down to its train for the morning run to Climax.

At 11:59 a.m. the same morning, Kindig found #641 pushing a string of flat cars just east of the Storke Portal. The Crusher plant is visible to the right.

The #641 is busy switching at the Storke Level of the Climax Molybdenum Mine at 2:19 p.m.

Engine #641 is switching at the Climax mill, in preparation for the afternoon's return to Leadville.

The late December afternoon sunlight shines on the #641, which has returned to the Leadville yard and is resting on the tie-up track beside the depot.

A winter storm has resulted in the services of the snowplow being required to open the line to Climax. The faithful rotary #99201, engine #641 and an icicle-covered wooden caboose are leaving Leadville on the cold morning of Feb. 11, 1960. By this date, scenes such as this have disappeared from every other American standard gauge railroad.
(Robert W. Richardson, Colorado Railroad Museum)

Another storm has plugged the High Line and the rotary is busy plowing just east of MP 140. This and the following photo is undated, but they were taken in the 1960s.
(Colorado Railroad Museum)

As the plow train works its way east, it passed near the site of the 1899 narrow gauge derailment at MP 139.7, shown on p. 40.

(Otto C. Perry, Denver Public Library, Western History Dept.)

In March 1955, Bob Richardson found the Climax Turn with four loads and two empties, just east of MP 140, two miles below the summit.

(Colorado Railroad Museum)

Rotary #99201 has arrived at the Climax yard. This big snow machine may be seen today at the Colorado Railroad Museum in Golden, Colo. It was a gift to the museum from the Burlington Northern Railroad. Date unknown.
(Otto C. Perry, Denver Public Library, Western History Dept.)

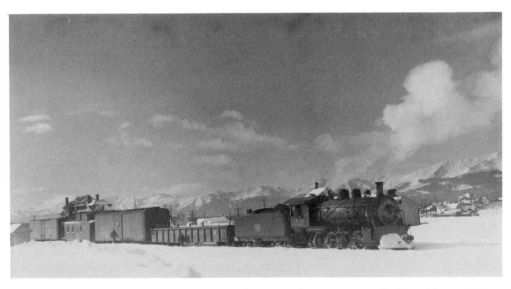

In the last year of steam operations on the C&S, the #641 is ready for a Climax Turn, Feb. 22, 1962. Every car in this train belongs to a railroad that no longer exists: CB&Q, New York Central and the Pennsylvania Railroad.   *(Richard H. Kindig)*

The #641 has just left the Leadville yard and is crossing Evans Gulch at MP 150.25. Feb. 22, 1962. (Richard H. Kindig)

LAST STEAM TRIP

The morning of Sept. 12, 1962 would at first appear to be like so many other late summer days in the Leadville yard, with #641 spotted on the coal track in preparation for the day's work on the line. However, when the #641 returned that afternoon from Climax, 78-1/2 years of steam railroading on the High Line came to an end. (Otto C. Perry, Denver Public Library, Western History Dept.)

The last C&S steam trip left the yard Sept. 12, 1962 with two beat-up gondolas and the caboose. Except for a few short industrial operations, there were no other standard gauge steam locomotives in regular service in the U.S. by this date. Otto Perry's trusty Ford is at the left.

On that same memorable trip, Perry found #641 along the large talus slope at MP 140.3, three miles out of Climax.

(Both photos, Otto C. Perry, Denver Public Library, Western History Dept.)

Westbound in the afternoon, the #641 rounds the curve at the headwaters of the Arkansas River, MP 138.7. Above the caboose are the remains of the John Reed mine, active so long ago during DSP&P ownership of the route. Ahead are the last twelve miles of service for engine #641.

(Otto C. Perry, Denver Public Library, Western History Dept.)

DIESELS ARRIVE ON THE HIGH LINE

When the diesel age arrived on the High Line in September 1962, the C&S assigned locomotive #828 to Leadville. An SD-9, it was built by the EMD Division of General Motors in January 1957. It received this red and white CB&Q paint scheme after an accident near Chugwater, Wyo. in September 1958. This photo was taken in Leadville, Sept. 14, 1968.

(Ed Fulcomer)

In stark contrast to the narrow gauge operations, #828 leaves Leadville June 19, 1978. After the merger of March 1970, the CB&Q became part of the new Burlington Northern (BN) Railroad. As part of the CB&Q, all C&S diesels were repainted BN green and black, with the small letters "C&S" just ahead of the cab.
(Ed Fulcomer)

In 1980 the C&S ceased operating as a separate company and all their engines were re-numbered. Thus #828 became #6223. After the French Gulch accident in June 1980 (p. 47), the #6223 required weeks of "intensive care" at Lincoln, Neb. When it was released, #6223 had received a more modern front end. The #6223 went back to Leadville and worked the Climax Turn until October 1986. It now works in yard service in Denver, Colo. and is shown here at 38th. Street, Dec. 14, 1986.
(Ed Fulcomer)

In her original Northern Pacific black and yellow paint job, is the future LC&S #1918. Built in August 1957, this GP-9 engine was used in freight service. After the Northern Pacific merged with the Burlington Northern in 1970, it became #1918. Location and date unknown.   (Henry Brueckmann. Collection of Ed Fulcomer)

Engine #1714 was working for the Burlington Northern at Bozeman, Mont. on July 29, 1976. This GP-9 locomotive was built for the Northern Pacific in August 1955 as #241 and was rebuilt in 1976 with the lowered nose it has today. No photo has been found of 1714 in its original colors.
(Ed Fulcomer)

REFERENCES

—————— BOOKS and ARTICLES ——————

Anonymous, 1886, Union Pacific Railway Co. Colorado Division, List of Bridges, Buildings and other Structures: Denver Public Library Western History Dept..

_____, 1894, Denver, Leadville & Gunnison Bridge and Structure Book: Denver Public Library, Western History Dept.

_____, 1923, Colorado & Southern Railway Co. List of Bridges, Trestles and Culverts. Chief Engineer's Office: Denver Public Library, Western History Dept.

_____, 1924 to 1978, Mineral Resources of the United States: U. S. Bureau of Mines, Washington, D.C.

_____, 1978, Travel the Routes of the Silver Kings: Leadville Chamber of Commerce, Leadville, Colo., 8 p.

_____, 1979, This is Climax Molybdenum: Amax, Inc., 24 p.

_____, 1982, Fryingpan-Arkansas Project: U. S. Bureau of Reclamation, Washington, D.C., 22 p.

Bauer, William H., Ozment, James L., and Willard, John, H., 1990, Colorado Post Offices, 1859-1989: Colorado Railroad Museum, Golden, Colo., 280 p.

Behre, C. H., Jr., 1953, Geology and Ore Deposits of the west slope of the Mosquito Range, Colorado: U.S. Geological Survey Professional Paper 235, 176 p.

Blair, Edward, 1972, Palace of Ice: Little London Press, Colorado Springs, Colo., 48 p.

_____, 1980, Leadville: Colorado's Magic City: Pruett Publishing Co., Boulder, Colo., 261 p.

Bryant, Bruce, Reed, Jack, Thompson, Tommy, Wallace, S. R., Karachewski, John, Sims, Paul, and Snow, Geoff, 1988, Geology and Mineral Resources of Central Colorado: Colorado Scientific Society Field Trip, 45 p.

Cafky, Morris, 1965, Colorado Midland: Rocky Mountain Railroad Club, Denver, Colo., 467 p.

Chappell, Gordon, Hauck, Cornelius, and Richardson, Robert W., 1974, The South Park Line—A Concise History: Colorado Railroad Museum, Annual No. 12, Golden, Colo., 280 p.

Collins, Donna Bishop, and Collins, Donley S., 1986, Scenic Trips into Colorado Geology: Lake County: American Institute of Professional Geologists Field Trip Guidebook, 41 p.

Colorado State Business Directories, 1877-1956.

Digerness, David S., 1977, The Mineral Belt, Vol. I, The Old South Park—Denver to Leadville: Sundance Publications, Ltd., Denver, Colo., 416 p.

_____, 1978, The Mineral Belt, Vol. II, The Old South Park—Across the Great Divide: Sundance Publications, Ltd., Denver, Colo., 416 p.

Ferrell, Mallory Hope, 1981, C&Sng Colorado & Southern Narrow Gauge: Pruett Publishing Co., Boulder, Colo., 238 p.

Gary, Margaret, Margaret, McAfee, Robert, Jr., and Wolf, Carol L., editors, 1972, Glossary of Geology: American Geological Institute, Washington, D.C. 805 p.

Griswold, Don , and Griswold, Jean, 1968, The Denver South Park & Pacific Builds the High Line: in Denver Posse of Westerners Brand Book, Denver, Colo., p. 296-322.

Henderson, Charles W., 1926, Mining in Colorado: U. S. Geological Survey Professional Paper 138, Washington, D. C., 263 p.

Hilton, George W., 1990, American Narrow Gauge Railroads: Stanford University Press, Stanford, Calif., 580 p.

Ingersoll, Ernest, 1883, Knocking Round the Rockies: Harper & Brothers, New York, N.Y., 220 p.

_____, 1888, The Crest of the Continent: A Record of a Summers's Ramble in the Rocky Mountains and Beyond: R. R. Donnelley & Sons, Chicago, Ill., 344 p.

Kindig, R. H., Haley, E. J., and Poor, M. C., 1959, Pictorial Supplement to Denver South Park & Pacific: Rocky Mountain Railroad Club, Denver, Colo., 467 p.

Koschmann, A. H., and Bergandahl, M. H., 1968, Principal Gold-producing Districts of the United States: U. S. Geological Survey Professional Paper 610, Washington, D. C., 283 p.

LeMassena, Robert A., 1974, Rio Grande to the Pacific: Sundance Publications, Ltd., Denver, Colo., 416 p.

Lovering, T. S., and Goddard, E. N., 1950, Geology and Ore Deposits of the Front Range, Colorado: U. S. Geological Survey Professional Paper 223, 319 p.

Nelson, R. A., 1970, Plants of Rocky Mountain National Park: Rocky Mountain Nature Association, Estes Park, Colo., 168 p.

Pesman, M. Walter, 1988, Meet the Natives, [8th Edition]: Denver Botanic Gardens, Denver, Colo., 237 p.

Poor, M. C., 1976, Denver South Park & Pacific, [Memorial Edition]: Rocky Mountain Railroad Club, Denver, Colo., 495 p.

Rische, C. W., 1991, personal communication

Smith, Duane A., 1989, Horace Tabor, His Life and Legend: University Press of Colorado, Boulder, Colo., 395 p.

Speas, Sam, and Coel, Margaret, 1985, Goin' Railroading: Pruett Publishing Co., Boulder, Colo., 312 p.

Thode, Jackson C., 1986, George L. Beam and the Denver & Rio Grande, Vol. I: Sundance Publications Ltd., Denver, Colo., 280 p.

Tweto, Ogden, 1968, Leadville district, Colorado in Ridge, J.D., ed., Ore deposits of the United States 1933-1967 (Graton-Sales Volume), v. 1: American Institute of Mining, Metallurgical and Petroleum Engineers, New York, NY, p. 681-713.

Voynick, Stephen M., 1984, Leadville: A Miner's Epic: Mountain Press Publishing Co., Missoula, Mont., 165 p.

Wagner, F. Hol, 1970, The Colorado Road: Intermountain Chapter, National Railway Historical Society, Inc., Denver, Colo., 415 p.

Weber, William A., 1976, Rocky Mountain Flora: Colorado Associated University Press, Boulder, Colo., 484 p.

Wilkins, Tivis E., 1974, Colorado Railroads: Pruett Publishing Co., Boulder, Colo., 309 p.

MAPS

Map of Leadville Mining District, Lake County, 1913, U. S. Geological Survey. Scale: 1 inch to 800 feet.

Sanders, Chas., S., 1901, Map of Leadville Mining District. No scale

Collins, Donna Bishop, and Collins, Donley S., 1986, Scenic Trips into Colorado Geology: Lake County. Geologic map covers Keystone, Silverthorne, Frisco, Copper Mountain, Leadville, Red Cliff, Minturn and Vail. Scale 1:100,000.

Tweto, Ogden, Moench, Robert H., and Reed, John C., Jr., 1978, Geologic Map of the Leadville Quadrangle, Northwestern Colorado: U. S. Geological Survey Map I-199, Miscellaneous Investigations Series. Scale: 1 inch to approx. 4 miles.

TIME TABLES
(Reprinted by the Colorado Railroad Museum)

The South Park Line, DL&G, August 1897

The Colorado Road, C&S Railway, April 1899

C&S Railway Co. Time Table No. 17, October 5, 1910

NEWSPAPERS

Griswold, Don, and Griswold, Jean, 1965-1971, Leadville a City of Contrast: in *The Leadville Herald Democrat.* A series of articles compiled from early-day Leadville newspapers. A detailed index of this collection of articles is on file at the Lake County Public Library, Leadville, Colo.

Leadville Daily Chronicle, April 30, 1879.

Leadville Herald Democrat, January-May, 1899; June-July, 1943.

The News Reporter, February-March, 1899.